The Complete
Law School
Companion

How to Excel at America's

Most Demanding

Post-Graduate Curriculum

Revised and Updated

JEFF DEAVER

John Wiley & Sons, Inc.

New York · Chichester · Brisbane · Toronto · Singapore

Library of Congress Cataloging-in-Publication Data

Deaver, Jeff.
    The complete law school companion : how to excel at America's most
  demanding post-graduate curriculum / Jeff Deaver. — 2nd ed.
      p.   cm.
    Includes index.
    ISBN 0-471-55491-X (alk. paper)
    1. Law—Study and teaching—United States.   I. Title.
KF283.D4   1992
340′.071′173—dc20   91-41666

ISBN 0-471-55491-X

Printed in the United States of America

10

To the memory of my grandfather,
Nelson W. Rider, Esq., sine qua non,
and, of course, for Helen

I hope to derive . . . something like a clew to guide us in our inquiries into what should be a proper education for a lawyer. And, in the first place, I find no one of the powers and faculties that Providence has given him which can be safely or harmlessly neglected. He will find use for them all; and, what is more, he will need them at all times in their full vigor and activity, to meet the demands which are made upon him, if he ever rises to the true dignity of the profession he has chosen.

Emory Washburn
The Study and Practice of Law

[W]hat is the orientation of the school with regard to the profession? What does it offer that you need? . . . To which the answer is: almost everything you will need for your practice.

Karl Llewellyn
The Bramble Bush

Contents

Preface to the
Second Edition

Since this book was first published in 1984, we have witnessed a number of significant changes in legal education and in the law itself.

The number of students applying to law school has slowed although the number of women and minority law students, in proportion to white male students, continues to grow. As the percentage of older and second-career law students increases and as a recession makes jobs scarce, law schools are moving away from a purely academic approach to study and are altering and expanding curricula to provide a practical legal education. Technology has made its way into the classroom and library in the form of laptop computers, video and audio tape study guides, computerized research, and CD-ROM hardware and databases.

Substantively, there have been changes in the *type* of law graduates practice. Wall Street mania is gone. The battlefield has shifted from boardrooms to bankruptcy courts. Insider-trading cases seem almost nostalgic—from pages of ancient legal history. New issues loom: abortion rights, homelessness, urban financing, prisoners' rights, and the use of public money to fund artistic projects. If the 1980s tested the creativity and stamina of commercial and corporate attorneys, the 1990s may very well be the era of constitutional and civil liberties lawyers, as the Bill of Rights is repeatedly put to the test.

Law firms are beginning to recognize that they can no

longer maintain a nineteenth-century mentality as we move toward the year 2000. They are, for instance, accommodating attorneys who wish to spend more time with their children and offering day-care arrangements and maternity *and* paternity leave. On the flip side, however, firms are quick to use newly learned cost-cutting management techniques and are much less reluctant to fire associates and even partners who do not live up to their standards of productivity.

With this realignment of the economy, the market for new attorneys in this early part of the decade is at a low point. While it may be easier to get into law school now than in 1984, finding the job you want upon graduation is going to be even harder than it was eight years ago. It is therefore all the more important to do well in school, not simply so that you will graduate near the top of your class but so that you can learn as much law as possible and use the three or four years ahead of you to their best advantage. Bringing your law school educational experience to this lofty level is the goal of the second edition of *The Complete Law School Companion*.

J. W. D.
New York City, 1991

Chapter One

⚖ An Introduction

*[For a glossary
of legal terms,
see Appendix Two.]*

Whether you're considering applying to law school, whether you've been accepted and are anxiously awaiting the first class session, or whether you're a second-year student who hasn't done quite as well as you'd hoped, you may feel that the legal profession is an intricate, incomprehensible puzzle that you'd like to be a part of—if only it weren't so, well, intricate and incomprehensible.

For all of you, I have good news and bad news.

The good news is that the material taught in law school is completely understandable by anyone with the intelligence to be accepted for admission in the first place. This is because law, unlike nuclear physics or biochemistry, is an institution regulating human activities on a very visible, familiar level. If you are aware of society itself, you can understand the subject matter of the law.

What's the bad news?

Consider just how many aspects of society must be regulated.

An example: Jane Doe, Esq., wakes up in the morning to her clock radio, makes coffee, heats rolls, and eats breakfast with her husband. She then takes the elevator to the lobby, says "Good morning" to the doorman, and leaves the building to dodge traffic on the way to the subway that will deliver her to downtown Manhattan, where she is a partner in a large law firm.

A simple scenario. But let's look at what a lawyer sees in those few facts:

- In the sale of the clock radio, coffee maker, and toaster oven, a lawyer would see federal and state trade regulations and antitrust laws, a state statute called the Uniform Commercial Code governing the sale of the appliances, and the law of negligence and products liability that would govern rights should the toaster, say, catch fire.
- In the food Ms. Doe and her husband ate for breakfast: the same rules as above, plus federal and state health regulations and statutes.
- In the gas and electricity in the apartment: state laws and regulations governing the sale and distribution of utility power.
- In Ms. Doe's relation with her husband: statutes and cases known as domestic relations law.
- In their apartment lease: the law of real property, contracts, housing and residential building codes, and landlord and tenant law.
- In their relation with the doorman: the law of agency.
- In the traffic on the street: state and city traffic laws, insurance law, negligence law, the Uniform Commercial Code again, consumer protection law, "lemon laws," and banking law (for financed cars).
- In Ms. Doe's law firm: partnership law, workers' compensation law, tax law, social security law, constitutional and antidiscrimination law, and general tort and contract law.

And working in conjunction with all of these laws is the body of procedural laws that govern how the courts enforce those other rights.

In sum, the bad news is simply this: Law may regulate everyday events, but it deals with a staggering number of them, and it does so in a very complex and detailed way. To be a successful lawyer you must differentiate among and organize all these rules and regulations; to be a successful student, you must do the same.

Two Keys to Success

When I was in school I found that success had little to do with intelligence or magic study techniques. The students who did well had two keys to success:

One, they were disciplined.

Two, they were good at organizing the mass of information they were taught.

The purpose of this book is to give you a technique for key number two—a system for organizing and processing all the information you get in your classes. I call this the Legal Concept Management (LCM) system.

If you follow the LCM techniques as I describe them, you will do well in law school. Very well. But that's a big "if," because the LCM approach requires a lot of work—as I mentioned, the other key to success is discipline, which *you* must provide. Either you're willing to work hard in law school or not. And if you're not, I can't do much for you. But if you want good grades, if you want to get the most out of law school, and if you're willing to work diligently, then this book can be of great help.

Why Bother?

You might ask yourself at this point: Why bother to do well in law school? You think: "I'm going to a good school. As long as I pass, I'll land a job. No problem." Well, sad to say, the world has changed from the days when your mothers and fathers went to law school. "Take-over" fever has become "take-cover" fever, and the number of plush jobs in classy firms has fallen in direct proportion to the clients who have gone under or cut back on operating expenses. While the number of students applying to law school seems to have stabilized, firms are being much more selective in their hiring and—what was unheard of as recently as ten years ago—are now firing attorneys who don't live up to their expected potential.

The short answer to the question "Why bother?" then is this: To get the job or clerkship you want.

By "job you want," however, I don't necessarily mean the most lucrative type of legal position. People choose law for reasons other than money, such as its potential for improving society, as a stepping stone to public office, or as a mentally stimulating way to spend the workday. If these are your goals, it is no less important to do well in school. Why? Because the most important, most interesting, and most rewarding legal jobs—whether they pay well or not—are avidly sought after by graduates. For instance, the Manhattan district attorney's office typically receives dozens of applications for each opening in the office. And that position pays about one-third the going rate in Wall Street firms. Similar competition is common at the Legal Aid Society and other public interest groups.

If you aren't attending a prestige law school, you will need to push a little harder than those students who are. I do not believe that these prestige schools produce better lawyers than other schools. But law firms in the process of hiring attorneys and judges hiring clerks often have a different view, and you may find a decided prejudice against graduates from nonprestige schools unless you can demonstrate through your individual academic performance that you are a potentially outstanding attorney.

Such self-interest isn't the only reason for doing well, however. In school, you are working *pro se,* as the legal expression goes—working for yourself only. In no time at all, though, you'll be representing clients who need your help. The attorney-client relationship is one of great trust. For these clients you are bound morally (and legally) to do all you can to solve their problems within the bounds of the law. You cannot represent clients half-heartedly; when their property, liberty, and even lives are at stake, you must make every effort on their behalf. Get accustomed to this attitude of hard work and diligence now; after all, you're only a few years away from becoming an attorney.

The LCM System

Now, what is this system that I'm claiming will catapult you to the head of your profession?

It's quite simple. The LCM system is a method for:

- Gathering information from class notes, digests of court cases (called "briefs"), and notes from outside of class.
- Creating a single master outline for each course.
- Using this outline and several other short lists in a very structured way to prepare yourself for the final exam.
- Taking the exam according to a highly effective method of analysis.
- Preparing class papers.

That's it. A lot of work, yes. But the results will be well worth the effort.

After we look at school selection and the law school admission process in the next several chapters, we'll tackle the stages in the LCM system:

LCM system I—classroom techniques

LCM system II—briefing cases

LCM system III—preparing a course outline

LCM system IV—preparing for and taking exams

LCM system V—preparing a course paper

Welcome to the world of legal study! The next three years will be like none other in your life.

And Keep in Mind . . .

The legal system: Appendix One is a brief overview of how the American legal system works. It is helpful to read this before you get too far into the LCM system.

Legal terms: Appendix Two is a glossary of legal terms a first-year law student should know. You may want to mark the first page of this Appendix with a paperclip or bookmark so you can refer to it whenever you come across a word in the text you aren't familiar with.

Second- and third-year students: This book is not just for beginning students. Any law student can use the LCM techniques to turn around a flagging academic showing. In addition, be sure to review Chapter 14; it contains a great deal of information just for upper-class students—including what courses to take and job interview techniques.

On using *The Complete Law School Companion:* Read
this book now—whether you're in school, an accepted applicant, an applicant still awaiting word on admission, or a potential student thinking about or planning to take the LSAT. Remember that both the study of law and the LCM system have
many gears and levers to master. Keep this book at hand
throughout your law school career and refer to it often.

Chapter Two

⚖ Is It for You?

Let's address a very legitimate question many of you may have: *Should* you go to law school? Of course, that's a question only you can answer, but I can help you do so by telling you in basic terms what a law degree can do for you.

First—forgive the apparent truism—it will let you practice law. Although it is still possible in a few states to be admitted to the bar by virtue of work experience, this is not a realistic possibility. If you wish to practice law, you must have a degree. This implies an even more basic question: Do you *want* to practice law?

My answer to this is to tell you about the rewards and drawbacks of the various types of legal practice in this country.

A second question to consider is: What kind of law school can you realistically expect to get into, and how will that affect your future career plans?

TYPES OF PRACTICE

Wall Street Firms

The name "Wall Street"—that very short avenue in Manhattan—is used not out of any geographic chauvinism, but rather because throughout the profession the term "Wall Street-type firm" has come to mean a large, more or less prestigious law firm representing major U.S. and foreign corporations, whether on LaSalle Street in Chicago, Market Street in San Francisco, or any other street in a city's financial district.

These firms are usually very large—while most of them

employ around 200 attorneys, some have more than 600. They specialize in the most sophisticated legal services available anywhere in the world, and currently charge their clients up to $400 an hour for their services (and even more for specialized work).

The litigation handled by these firms is often massive. Huge corporate lawsuits may last seven, eight, even nine years from the time the suit is originally filed until the date it is ultimately resolved. On the nonlitigation side of the business, these firms represent their clients in multimillion-dollar business transactions, orchestrating corporate acquisitions and takeovers, issuing stocks and bonds, or lending billions of dollars.

The Wall Street firm is segmented into specialty groups: litigation, corporate, real estate, trusts and estates, and sometimes such specialties as antitrust, entertainment, labor, admiralty, aviation, and food and drug law.

A partnership is the usual business structure of these firms (as opposed to, say, a corporation), which means that there are a number of owners (the "partners"), who both manage the firm and are responsible to the clients for the legal work. The employed attorneys are called "associates."

Associates spend most of their first year or so doing research for partners or senior associates on a wide variety of legal questions, often rotating from one department to another. They also write simple legal documents or—more likely—small portions of very complicated documents, proofread, carry partners' files for them on business trips, oversee the mechanical aspects of getting documents in proper form, and in general serve as assistants whenever needed.

Is the work interesting?

It can be, especially if you like the challenge of library research or the excitement of being a part of a multimillion-dollar international business transaction. In the whole, however, much of an associate's work can be dreadfully dull. And the hours can be excruciating—an associate may have to work through the night, 24 hours straight, on occasion.

But there are compensations. First, you won't be enduring drudgery for long. In a few years, you'll be doing small deals of your own. Second—I suspect you guessed this one—you'll be paid a great deal of money. This year, first-year associates in Manhattan were making about $90,000. And if you're at all capable, that figure will rise appreciably every year.

It used to be that an attorney would be hired either out of law school or from another firm and after about eight years' experience he or she would be evaluated by the partners with an eye toward inviting that attorney to join the firm; being named partner has been the ultimate goal of most attorneys seeking work in a large firm. Attorneys who were "passed over" by the partnership (i.e., not invited to become a "member of the firm") would generally leave the firm.

While this procedure is still generally true, changes in the economy and in the mentality of firms have given rise to different systems. Many people—particularly working parents—who enjoy practicing law do not want the responsibility or the hours required to become and to remain a partner, and firms are finding that they must be creative in developing alternative working environments if they want to retain talented attorneys. Sometimes, if an associate is not asked to become partner, that attorney is given the option of staying on as a permanent associate. Some firms are experimenting with a tiered partnership arrangement, which confers varying rights and responsibilities on different levels of partners. Some attorneys are hired with the understanding that they are not interested in competing for a partnership slot.

The formula for making partner is complicated and largely unwritten. Among the factors tossed into the hopper are:

- legal knowledge and experience
- compatibility with fellow partners
- area of specialty
- ability to bring business into the firm
- relationship with clients
- certain social graces (although firms may deny using this criterion)

If you do make it to partner, you'll very likely find yourself in a job that will pay you well over $300,000 a year and will get you home by seven or eight every evening, leaving some—

although not all—weekends free. (The present economic climate, however, has kept even senior partners scurrying about looking for new clients and maintaining their own billable hours to keep revenue pouring into the firm coffers.)

Wall Street-type firms have also been a breeding ground for politicians. If you have your eye on the White House or Capitol Hill, it can do you no harm to start making contacts through a major law firm.

Small Urban Firms

Wall Street-type firms represent the major corporations and banks in this country. But many corporations and individuals can't afford their services and don't need their high-power legal talent. It is the small law firms located in or near cities that service such clients.

The nature of the work is similar to that of the larger firms—mostly corporate law and litigation—although small urban firms tend not to do much of the large antitrust, tender offer (a type of corporate acquisition), and financing work of the larger firms. But the principles are the same; only the scope is smaller. Like the large firms, these have partners and associates (generally between 20 and 100 attorneys altogether). Your chances for becoming a partner will probably be somewhat better at a smaller firm because there is more room to expand. In many smaller firms, hours tend to be shorter, but the pay is less than at the large firms. And you won't have the abundant support staff and technology (computers, libraries, and continuing education programs, for instance) that large firms provide.

These smaller firms tend to offer more personal or individual legal services (wills, trusts, divorces, personal injury advice and litigation, and house and condo closings, for instance) than larger firms. If you wish to specialize in one of these areas, a smaller urban firm might be for you.

One- or Two-Attorney Practices

Law offices with one or two attorneys have largely gone the way of general practice physicians (the ones who used to make house calls, remember?). Certainly in the areas of general corporate law, financing law, and large litigation, an individual attorney cannot hope to compete with a large firm—the cost of the support equipment and staff is prohibitive. But apart from such areas of practice, an attorney who is able to build up a clientele (or take over an existing clientele from a retiring attorney) can establish a successful practice.

Don't count on a huge income, and don't expect the hours to be shorter. Solo lawyers work very hard, and because their clients are usually working people, conferences are often held at night and on weekends. Moreover, if you're the only one running the show, vacations present obvious problems. Solo practitioners who specialize in litigation also find themselves spending much time doing nonproductive (and, therefore, nonrevenue-producing) tasks, such as sitting around the courthouse waiting for calendar calls.

Still many people are quite attracted to the notion of having their own practice, and I do know of several young attorneys who, after a few years of practice with a large firm, begged or borrowed money to hang out their shingle. They specialize in landlord-tenant law, residential real estate, immigration law, and divorces. After a brief period of struggle, they now have solid client bases and, although they don't entertain at Maxim's or Lutece, have sufficient job satisfaction so that they consider themselves more than adequately compensated.

Government Law Practice

Federal, state, and city governments hire many attorneys. The most visible of these are, of course, the prosecuting attorneys who represent the state or federal government in criminal actions. Probably nowhere will you get as much trial experience as quickly as by prosecuting criminal cases.

These lawyers (called "state's attorneys," "district attorneys," or "attorneys general") usually have their choice of specializing in trials or appellate argument (see Appendix One for a discussion of the distinction).

The drawbacks? Money is one. This year, assistant district attorneys (ADAs), the starting position in Manhattan for prosecutors, earned salaries of $30,000 a year ($31,000 upon admission to the bar). That is roughly what a good, experienced legal secretary in the Big Apple might make. There is also a "burn-out factor" among these lawyers. Beyond a certain time, usually four or five years, the rewards and learning benefits are outweighed by the low income and lack of variety in the job. Finally, prosecuting jobs are extremely competitive. Recently, the Manhattan district attorney's office received 2,700 applications for 60 openings. And many of those seeking the jobs were top graduates from prestige schools.

The state's attorney's office and the U.S. attorney's office are not limited to handling criminal cases. They, along with attorneys working for specialized agencies in the state and federal system, also handle civil suits involving the government as a party. For instance, a contractor enters a contract with the state to build a road, but doesn't complete the job on time. The state—just like any individual or business—can sue for this breach. But this isn't a criminal matter; it's a *civil* lawsuit, and the state will be represented by one of its own attorneys in this action.

To give you an idea of the variety of governmental legal jobs and how they relate to individual functions of government, consider these departments in which you, a young attorney, seeking a job with New York State, might practice:

- criminal prosecution
- civil rights
- antitrust
- consumer fraud protection
- general litigation
- trusts and estates
- labor
- mental hygiene

In addition to these you might choose the legal office of a specific agency of the state: the Department of Taxation and

Finance, the Environmental Conservation Department, the Secretary of State's office, or the Department of Insurance.

Corporations

All large corporations and many small ones employ attorneys in their corporate legal departments, supervised by the company's general counsel, or chief attorney. The rising cost of outside legal services (remember that $400-an-hour figure?) and the fact that much corporate law is straightforward have led to the recent growth of such departments.

In companies with small legal departments the legal staff serves as liaison between the company's executives and the outside law firm and does the simpler legal work. In large departments, the corporate attorneys do the bulk of the company's legal work and rely on outside counsel only for specialties—antitrust matters, tender offers, bond offers, stock issuances, and large litigation.

In-house attorneys, as they are called, are well paid—they earn less than Wall Street lawyers, but receive more in perks: stock options, profit sharing plans, and retirement plans. In-house counsel jobs are also good springboards from which to move into management of the corporation itself.

The major problem with this type of practice is that it can be dreadfully routine; the good, challenging work gets farmed out to firms. There will also be fewer opportunities to go to court. And, if you go directly from school to a corporation, you will be less professionally mobile than if you first work in a law firm. In other words, it is difficult to go from a corporation to a prestige firm, but easy to do the opposite. (It is, in fact, quite common for associates who are not chosen to be partners to leave their firms and take a job with a corporation client they had been representing.)

A final disadvantage is that legal departments in corporations are structured on the pyramid principle. There is one boss—the general counsel. If you are ambitious, you're going to find yourself standing in line with maybe 30 other ambitious, talented lawyers, waiting for that job to open up. A law firm, on the other hand, can simply grow to accommodate new partners.

Public Service

By public service I don't mean politics, but rather a legal career with a nonprofit organization or other group dedicated to the benefit of the public or a particular segment of society.

Some of these organizations have a specific purpose other than providing legal services for their members (e.g., the NAACP or Planned Parenthood). Others function solely as a mechanism to provide legal help to those who need but can't afford it (such as the Legal Aid Society).

To give you an idea of what public interest law is, consider the New York Legal Aid Society, which employs hundreds of full-time attorneys. Examples of the services provided to more than 200,000 persons each year are the following: class-action suits contesting the failure of city agencies to provide the poor with adequate emergency housing and assistance in locating permanent housing, child custody cases, challenges to the denial of social services and benefits, consumer protection litigation, and defending indigents accused of crimes.

The pros and cons of these jobs are obvious: superb experience (in a recent year, each Criminal Division Legal Aid lawyer handled about 400 cases!) and the spiritual rewards of working for a cause that you believe in. The negatives are the low pay and the limited potential these jobs have as long-term careers.

You should also be aware of a couple other aspects of these jobs, one bad and one good. First, they're not easy to come by. Even in Manhattan, where overhead is as high as in any city in the country, young lawyers—many of them top graduates from prestige schools—are standing in line for such jobs. Funding cutbacks have hit public service legal programs particularly hard.

Second, on a more positive note, although the work may sound unimportant, public service attorneys have traditionally been on the cutting edge of making major changes in American society. Often, it is not a Wall Street firm but a young public service attorney who takes on a case that re-defines the U.S. Constitution and safeguards personal free-doms. It is entirely conceivable that even as a newly admitted attorney you might find yourself arguing a case before the Supreme Court, an honor very few Wall Street partners have had.

Keep in mind that if you're a public-spirited sort but find a public service career financially beyond your means, all large firms offer their attorneys a chance to take on cases of a "pro bono" nature (from the Latin *pro bono publico*—"for the pub-lic good"). These are, in effect, charity cases taken on by firms for free. (Don't worry—you'll still get your paycheck; the law firm foots the bill!)

Nonlegal Careers

What if you don't intend to practice law? Should you still go to law school?

This question isn't as curious as you may think. Many peo-ple feel that a law degree will help them in business or poli-tics. If you're thinking of a non-practicing career, consider the following:

Remember that the cost of a legal education is high. Tuition at prestige schools is hovering around $17,000 this year. Add to that the absence of income from the job you would have had if you had not gone to law school, and you can see that the ultimate cost of a legal education can be astronomical—perhaps as much as a $125,000.

If you practice law at a medium-sized or large firm, this expense will be recouped fairly quickly. Say that your first job, at a medium-sized firm, pays $80,000, which is slightly less than this year's going rate on Wall Street and perhaps $45,000 more than your salary at the job you might have had if you'd started working right out college. Setting aside such factors as inflation or tax differentials, in about three or four years you will have recouped the cost of your education.

But let's say you go to law school at that cost of $125,000 and never practice, but work in a company where you get a slightly better income (let's say $7,000 more a year) because of your law degree. It will take you roughly 15 or more years to recoup this expense. And if you become a sales manager or computer scientist or painter, you'll swallow the whole cost of that education.

However, let's say you're looking for some way to delay the inevitable—that moment when you have to get your first job and fly the nest. You think of law school and find a state college where tuition is nominal or your uncle, the late Judge Jones, leaves you $60,000 on condition that you use it for tuition.

Should you do it?

On a personal level, law school will give you an education in human nature and the mechanics of modern American society as no other course of study can. (In addition to being an attorney, I am a novelist of suspense fiction—murder mysteries—and I can say without qualification that my law school education was as valuable for that avocation as all of the writing and literature courses I've ever taken.)

Simply surviving the three years will build up your confidence, get your analytical abilities in high gear, accustom you to thinking and speaking on your feet, and raise the eyebrows of the people you deal with both professionally and personally.

Very well and good. But nobody's going to plunk down 60 grand just for some insights into human nature, are they? What's the bottom line? This: If you plan to go into business for yourself or work for either a small company or a large one in an executive capacity, law school can provide you with invaluable information on business practices, taxation, and your rights and obligations in professional or corporate America. A one-semester course in business law, taught at a business school, cannot give you this kind of education.

If, on the other hand, you aim for, say, a selling career, financial analysis, medicine, stock brokerage, art, computer science, or engineering, it might be in your best interest to save the tuition money and get down to work doing what you want to do. Law will probably not help you sufficiently to justify the time and expense.

THE QUALITY OF YOUR SCHOOL

Another factor affecting your decision to apply to law school is the quality of those schools that you realistically think you can get into or of those that do, in fact, accept you. The question comes down to this: Should you invest the time and money if the only school that will accept you is Sam's Correspondence Law School & Bartending Course?

The Myth of the Prestige School

In few areas of education is the hierarchy of schools as evident as in law. Unabashed prejudices in favor of or against certain schools exist; you'll discover this as soon as you start the job interview process during your second or third year. Like all prejudices, of course, these are wildly subjective (preferring Harvard to Yale, for instance). Nor are they cast in stone. Just because a hiring partner is in love with Harvard (her alma mater), this does not mean that a Boston University grad will never get a job at that firm. I am speaking here about tendencies.

Any accredited law school will give you a sufficient education to qualify you to be a lawyer if you do the required work. Don't think that you can't practice law just because you didn't attend one of the top ten. Law is law; its principles operate independently of what is taught in school. (You will occasionally find, in fact, a prejudice *against* the prestige schools because they tend to neglect the nuts and bolts of practice in favor of a theoretical perspective.)

The reality is this: There are more graduates from law school than there are jobs for them. If you attend a prestige school and do very well, you can—even in today's inflated marketplace—just about write your own ticket. If you attend a local, nonprestige law school and do very well (top 10 percent), you will have much the same job opportunities–large firms, clerkships, attractive government jobs—as your prestige-school counterpart, but only in the area in which the school is located.

ABA-Approved Schools

One aspect of your selection of school is vitally important: whether the schools you are considering are approved by the American Bar Association.

There are presently 176 law schools in this country approved by the American Bar Association and approximately 37 law schools that have not been approved. ABA approval status means that a graduate from that school meets the law school education requirements for admission to the bar in all states (there are other requirements for admission, of course, the bar exam being not the least). Graduating from a nonapproved school does not necessarily mean you cannot practice law. Some states permit non-ABA-approved-school graduates to sit for the bar exam in that particular state, but usually they are not permitted to take the exam in other jurisdictions.

It is vitally important to know whether the schools you are applying to are ABA-approved or not. If not, you should explore how attending such a school will affect your ability to practice law after graduation. Talk to the schools, the state bar association, and the board of bar examiners in the state in which the school is located.

Questions about ABA approval can be addressed to:

The American Bar Association
Consultant's Office
Indiana University School of Law
550 West North Street
Indianapolis, IN 46202

The Grade Game

Well, what about those students who graduate from an approved school, but who have less-than-attractive academic records? Those who attended prestige schools are still going to get job offers from some big firms. Those who did not attend such schools will—if they have a reasonably good academic record—get offers from small firms and corporate legal departments. Those with low grades from local schools will sometimes look for a long time before they find their first job.

And when they do, it may not be in their preferred subject or locale.

Therefore, if you are accepted only by Sam's Law School, you should plan to attend only if you are willing to work like crazy to push yourself to the top of the class.

Get Off the Fence

Finally, keep in mind that your author is prejudiced (an "interested witness," a lawyer would say). Law is more than a job or a career. It gets into you; it makes absurd mental, emotional, and even physical demands on you. But it pays you very well, and it does so in whatever currency you want: money, excitement, fascination, the satisfaction of helping others. If you want a profession that is something you *are*, and not just something you *do*, then write out that nonrefundable application fee check, stick it in the envelope sitting on your dresser (where it's been for the last indecisive month), and turn to the next chapter of this book.

Chapter Three

♊ The Admission Process: The LSAT and Other Hurdles

Applying to law school is like preparing for an invasion; you must have strategy and foresight. You must get started early, selecting the schools you would like to attend (and backup schools that you would be *willing* to attend if you are rejected by your first choices), lining up financial aid for tuition and expenses, starting the application process, arranging for living quarters, and so on.

You're Not Alone

Although the number of students applying to law school has stabilized over the past several years, there are still many more applicants than there are spots in first-year classes, especially at the best schools. In 1990, more than a half-million applications were submitted to U.S. law schools. When you consider that there are only about 200 law schools in the country (combining ABA-approved and nonapproved schools) you can see that the sheer volume of applications is staggering. Applicants are considered on the basis of many factors, undergraduate performance and scores on the Law School Admissions Test (LSAT)[1] being the two main criteria. Some-

---

[1] "LSAT" is a registered trademark of Law School Admission Services, Inc.

21

times "soft" factors like work experience and the impression made during personal interviews may be taken into consideration.

Plan Early

It is vital that you contact the schools you are interested in attending to find out their requirements as soon as possible. Many schools have deadlines that are earlier than you might expect. Also the LSAT is offered only four times a year. Early planning is necessary to make sure schools have all the data they need by their deadlines.

THE LAW SCHOOL ADMISSION COUNCIL/ LAW SCHOOL ADMISSION SERVICES

A not-for-profit organization known as the Law School Admission Council, an association of American and Canadian schools, facilitates and standardizes the law school admission process. An affiliate of the council, the Law School Admission Services (LSAS), provides several services you should know about.

1. LSAS administers the LSAT examination.

2. LSAS assembles and provides schools with each student's undergraduate transcripts and other data through the Law School Data Assembly Service (LSDAS). Nearly all law schools require their applicants to use the LSDAS, which summarizes, standardizes, and compiles various types of information: LSAT scores, academic records at other schools (including law schools), biographical information, and special material (such as correspondence regarding handicaps or conditions under which tests were taken). This report is then sent to the law schools the applicant has specified. The report may also include an admissions index—a mathematical formula that combines the LSAT score and grade point into a single number.

3. LSAS operates the Candidate Referral Service (CRS), which allows—with your permission—a law school to search

the LSAS files for applicants who might have certain criteria sought by that school for its student makeup. For instance, a school may wish to recruit students with certain geographic backgrounds, grade point averages, or economic backgrounds. The LSAS reports that schools sometimes contact applicants with such characteristics directly even if the students themselves had not considered applying to that school.

4. LSAS administers a loan program for students, the Law Access[2] program. Under this plan, students who are attending ABA-approved law schools that are members of the Law School Admission Council may apply for one of several loans to meet the cost of attending law school.

5. LSAS provides a number of helpful publications for current law students and those thinking of applying to law school.

THE LSAT EXAM

Of the more than 200 ABA-approved and nonapproved law schools in the United States, virtually every one requires that its applicants take the LSAT.[3] According to the Law School Admission Council, 150,000 LSATs were administered in 1990. The council goes on to explain the reasoning behind the test:

> The LSAT is designed to measure skills that are considered essential for success in law school: the ability to read and comprehend complex texts with accuracy and insight, organize and manage information and draw reasonable inferences from it, reason critically, and analyze and evaluate the reasoning and argument of others.

[2] "Law Access" is a registered trademark of Law School Admission Services, Inc.

[3] Please note that all information presented here about the exam and the other services of the Law School Admission Council and the Law School Admission Services was provided by them in the summer of 1991. Legal education changes slowly, but it does sometimes change. Be sure to contact these organizations directly for specific information on their programs before you take the exam and apply to law school. Their address is found at the end of this chapter.

This standardized test was changed several years ago. It is now made up of five sections (each 35 minutes long) of multiple-choice questions and one writing sample (30 minutes long). The multiple-choice questions have been limited to three categories: reading comprehension, analytical reasoning, and logical reasoning. Generally only four of the five sections are used in computing the applicant's score; the fifth section is used to sample new types of test questions that might be used in future LSAT exams.

Traditionally, the test is offered in June, October, December, and February at selected locations around the country. When the test falls on a Saturday, the LSAS has in the past offered an alternative day for those applicants who observe Saturday sabbaths. In addition, special test-taking arrangements are available for handicapped students and those who must take the test at a location other than one of those normally scheduled.

If, after taking the exam, you believe you tested poorly, you may cancel the score by contacting the LSAS immediately (they must receive the cancellation notice no later than five working days after the test date). The LSAS reports, however, that—barring some major catastrophe in taking the test the first time—retaking the test will usually result at best in only a slight improvement in your score. But if for some reason your mind goes blank or you are hit with a bout of flu or amnesia midway through the exam, you have a mechanism by which to void the results of that particular test.

The LSAT application booklet (see ordering information at the end of this chapter) details in depth the procedure for preparing for and taking the exam. This booklet contains sample questions and answers and a sample test. In addition, the LSAS offers several publications to assist you in preparing for the test. Preparation guides (including complete sample tests) and preparation courses are offered by companies not affiliated with the LSAS or the council. They are similar to the commercial bar exam review services and publications. We don't have the space here to offer a sample exam (total pretest, test, and post-test time is estimated by the LSAS to be about seven hours!), but I will mention briefly the categories of questions that have been used in the past.

Reading Comprehension

You will be presented with four passages, each about 450 words long (roughly equal to two double-spaced typed pages of information). Following each passage will be five to eight questions about each passage. Although this is a *law school* admissions test, the questions might or might not be about the law. The subject matter may be any topic at all, including science, philosophy, and the humanities. Remember, this portion of the exam does not test your knowledge of the various subjects (if you know something about the topics beforehand, you should still rely only on what is in the written passage before you); it measures your ability to comprehend what you have read and, according to the LSAS, "to draw reasonable inferences from the material in the passage."

You will have 35 minutes to complete the reading comprehension passage.

Analytical Reasoning Problems

These multiple-choice questions test your ability to deduce certain facts about the relationship among people, things, places, and so on, from certain given information. These questions are also known as "games," and in fact are similar to the word problems found in books of games or magazines. They give some indication of your ability to analyze relationships among events and entities in practice, and to draw logical conclusions.

Here's a very simple example of this type of reasoning problem:

These are given conditions:

- *Roe, Doe, Jones, and Fred frequent a certain bar where Smith has been shot.*
- *Roe and Smith are never in the bar together.*
- *Jones and Smith are always in the bar together.*
- *Either Doe or Jones, but not both, will be in the bar.*
- *When Fred is in the bar, either Smith or Roe, but not both, will be in the bar too.*

Who were the witnesses to Smith's shooting?

    a. Roe, Doe, and Fred
    b. Jones and Fred
    c. Doe, Jones, and Fred
    d. Only Fred
    e. Only Jones

The answer is b. We can deduce that Doe and Roe will not be witnesses to the shooting but Jones and Fred will be.

The answer is easy when you draw a square representing the bar and put Smith inside, and go through the set of givens one by one. If Smith is in the bar, Roe will not be, so put him outside the bar. Similarly if Smith is in the bar, Jones will be, so put him inside. If Jones is inside, as he is, therefore Doe will not be. Since Roe is outside the bar, and Smith is inside, then Fred is inside too.

Please note that this is merely an example of the *type* of analytical reasoning that the examiners test for. The actual LSAT questions are in a different form.

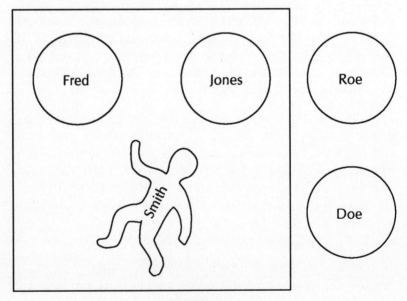

Figure 1.

The analytical reasoning section is also timed at 35 minutes.

Logical Reasoning

The LSAT presents two sections on logical reasoning. The sections, also referred to as the "arguments" sections, present a short body of text and then ask you to perform one of several types of reasoning:

- identify the central point of the passage
- identify assumptions upon which an argument is based
- draw a conclusion from premises
- detect errors in reasoning

For instance, you may be asked to select the answer that is the closest to the author's main purpose, to describe the author's attitude toward a passage of text, to make inferences from the passage, or to resolve apparently conflicting statements.

The LSAS states that while applicants need not know the terminology of formal logic, they are expected to understand "widely used concepts such as 'argument,' 'premise,' 'assumption,' and 'conclusion.'"

Here's an example of the type of logical reasoning you would be expected to perform:

A group of sociologists has found that the majority of felons arrested for violent crimes in a particular inner city neighborhood are illiterate. A newspaper article reported that the neighborhood's crime rate for felonies decreased last year. Therefore, the article concluded, a greater percentage of the population of the neighborhood is able to read, compared with the year before.

Is this conclusion correct?

The answer is that the newspaper's conclusion is wrong. There is no proof of a causal relationship between committing, and being arrested for, felonies and illiteracy. There could still be a growing number of nonfelons who cannot read.

Again, let me stress that the above example is not in the exact form of an LSAT question. But it does give you an idea of the type of logical reasoning that the examiners are looking for.

There are two logical reasoning sections on the test, timed for a total of one hour and ten minutes (they are broken down into two 35-minute segments).

The Writing Sample

The final section of the LSAT requires you to write an essay on a preselected topic. It is not graded for the purposes of your LSAT score; the sample will be included in the information sent by the LSDAS to the schools of your choice.

The one word of advice is this: Do not start writing immediately! As with law school exams, you must first organize and do a brief outline of your essay (scratch paper should be provided by the proctors). Think about what you are going to write before you put pen to paper. Organization and clarity are far more important than volume.

You will have 30 minutes to complete this portion of the test.

CHOOSING A SCHOOL

As you fill out your application for the LSAT, you'll have to indicate which schools should receive test reports. Keep in mind, as you are leafing through catalogs and scheduling interviews, that choosing a law school is a fundamentally different process than choosing a school for undergraduate study. While you'll find that the subjects covered in one law school are—on paper, at least—identical to those taught in any other, it is also true that each school has a different slant and reputation. Some schools, for instance, boast a high percentage of graduates going on to local and state government office. Some produce craftsmanlike, business-oriented attorneys, while others have a greater percentage of public-interest graduates than other schools. Some breed academicians who go on to become professors and legal philosophers, articulating, describing, and even creating the rights that other lawyers enforce.

There is only one way for you to learn the flavor of the schools you are considering applying to: investigate them. Go to the campus, walk around, take tours, talk to students, talk to graduates, talk to faculty members. Read local directories of attorneys, judges, and politicians; see which law schools they went to. If your goal is to land a job in a big firm in a particular city, find out if a particular school has spawned a greater percentage of partners in the large firms around town than any other school.

Be a Detective

There is another reason to visit the schools: to observe the real (the good and the bad) characteristics of a school, traits that aren't evident on a tour or in an interview. While it's almost universally true that there are more applicants than openings at most law schools, there are far fewer *perfect* applicants than schools would like. A law school is a business. It succeeds when it produces hard-working, knowledgeable students, who in turn move successfully into the workplace. Schools therefore engage in a fair amount of "selling" themselves to those individuals who seem as if they will be successful students, enhancing the school's own reputation.

In short, a pretty catalog does not a good school make.

Be skeptical. Walk around the campus. See if you can sit in on a few classes. Grade the school on the following:

- Are professors late for class or absent?
- What resources are available?
- Is there only one Lexis computer terminal for the entire school?
- How many law reviews and other legal journals does the school publish? (The more the better.)

- How many copies of each case reporter does the library have? (You can bet that if a professor suggests to his class of 200 that they take at look at *Gnome* v. *Troll,* and the case is reported in only one book, you're going to be standing in line a long, long time.)
- Is the library a shambles? Or is it clean and orderly?
- Are students complaining about missing books?
- Are classrooms so crowded students must sit in the aisles, or so poorly attended that the professor is speaking to a handful of those registered for the course?

You will be spending a vast amount of time in the hallowed halls of your law school; you owe it to yourself to make sure it is the kind of place in which you will feel comfortable.

A Reminder:

—Act early to begin the law school admission process. It will take more time and effort than when you applied to undergraduate school.

—Contact the Law School Admission Council/Law School Admission Services as soon as possible to find out about the LSAT, the LSDAS, and their other services. Write to:

Law Services
Box 2000
661 Penn Street
Newtown, PA 18940-0998

Chapter Four

⚖ Mysteries Revealed: What's Law School Really Like?

Those of you in your second semester and beyond or those with older brothers or sisters who have given you the scoop on law school will find that this chapter really isn't for you. It's for those of you who are approaching law school the same way you'd ride through a dark tunnel on a roller coaster—confident, but you'd feel just a little bit more comfortable knowing what lurks ahead.

Avoiding the Stumble Syndrome

One of the biggest problems facing law students in their early weeks is the "stumble syndrome." This malady occurs because students are hit with so much new information—and hit so quickly—during the first month of school that they feel they are continually stumbling from day to day, unable to find any firm footing.

The result of this syndrome is that students take so long to get oriented to the *ways* of law school itself that they don't start learning what law school is supposed to teach them (i.e., the rules of law) until they're already behind. So if you know what to expect, you'll be able to hit the decks running and get down to the business of learning law much sooner. And the first thing you've got to learn about is the Socratic method of teaching.

THE CLASSROOM APPROACH—THE SOCRATIC METHOD

What will your daily life in law school be like? Perhaps the most striking initial observation you'll make about your first-year law classes is their size. Typical classes contain between 100 and 150 students.

Although you've all undoubtedly taken large lecture courses in undergraduate school, you cannot compare law school and undergraduate classes because most law professors don't lecture. They use some variation on what's called the "case method" or Socratic approach to education, in which they call on an individual student and ask questions about the material assigned for that day.

So while you may feel safe and complacent surrounded by 149 other faces, you're going to be a lot more vulnerable to cross-examination by your law school professor than you ever were in undergrad school.

The Socratic method is not new, nor is it unique to law school. In fact, only recently (in the last 100 years; and that, in law, is recent) and only in the United States has the technique been applied to the study of law. Prior to the late 1800s, law was learned through the reading of treatises and commentaries written by judges and practitioners and through on-the-job training.

Here's a brief example of the Socratic method in action:

There is a rule of law called "assumption of risk," which holds that if you see a clear danger and go ahead and take the risk of getting hurt, you might not be able to win a suit against the person who created that danger.

There. That's a rule of law. Simple and concise, understandable and fair. But your torts professor isn't going to recite the rule as I just did. The professor will try to draw it out of you, to make *you* figure it out.

Consider this brief exchange:

PROFESSOR: Imagine there's a bridge spanning a river. You walk across it and halfway over the cables break. You fall into the water and are seriously injured. What would you do about it?

STUDENT: Sue the owner of the bridge.

PROFESSOR: On what grounds?

STUDENT: Negligence. If the bridge was open, the cables should have been strong enough to hold a pedestrian's weight.

PROFESSOR: What if, before you crossed, you noticed that the cables were frayed?

STUDENT: I must not have thought they were too bad if I crossed.

PROFESSOR: No, you thought they were very badly frayed. But you had a vitally important appointment across the river you could not miss. What would the owner of the bridge claim in court?

STUDENT: That I was negligent too?

PROFESSOR: Negligence is carelessness. You weren't careless. You were stupid. You *saw* the danger and decided to act pigheaded. You crossed a dangerous bridge anyway. . . . How would you describe what you did?

STUDENT: I took a chance.

PROFESSOR: You took a *what*?

STUDENT: I took a chance, a risk. . . .

PROFESSOR: Ah, a risk. You took a risk. . . . What else might you have done with that risk? Think of a lawyerly word, a big word. . . .

STUDENT: I *assumed* the risk.

PROFESSOR: Very good.

See how the rule was drawn out by the professor?

In law school, the system will probably work this way: Your assignments will consist of court decisions, usually contained in a casebook in which the author has compiled a number of decisions, each one representing a rule of law that you're to learn.

You'll read these cases—maybe four, six, or eight for each class session—and then "brief" them, that is, write a short synopsis of the cases according to the process described in the next chapter.

You show up in class the next day and prop open your notebook containing the briefs and your notebook for class notes.

Then the fun begins.

The professor may give a brief introduction to the topic you are about to cover and then call on a student. Or the professor may simply pick a name and begin the Socratic process cold.

You will usually be asked to recite the facts of the decision and possibly the procedural history of the case as it worked its way through the court system. Once you have finished, the professor may allow you to continue, discussing the rule of law and any other observations you may have made during your reading of the decision.

If you correctly state the facts and the rule of law that the case represents, that might be the end of it. Often, though, the professor will let you recite just long enough until you have enough rope. Then the professor will open the trap door—and start the questioning.

Professors usually ask straightforward queries about the facts and the rule of the law the court selected. Also: "Why?" Get used to that question. Law school professors love it. Even if you're positive you know all the facts cold, even if you can recite the rule of law in your sleep, be prepared for a professor's ironic glance, accompanied by "But *why* did the court do that?" Or "*Why* did the attorney representing the plaintiff bring the case in this court and not another?"

Socratic sessions require you to shift gears quickly. It's not unusual for you to be reciting a case when suddenly the professor interrupts you, changes the facts, and asks you to offer what the rule of law might be if *those* facts, rather than the ones in the case, existed. The professor might state a different legal rule, then ask you to apply *that* to the facts in the case you briefed for class. You will often be asked to reconcile the decision you have just recited with previous cases.

Here's another example of a Socratic professor at work:

PROFESSOR: Ms. Jones?
STUDENT: Yes, sir? Present.
PROFESSOR: Please stand and tell us about the case of *Brown* v. *Smith*.
STUDENT: Yes, well, in this case, a young man . . .
PROFESSOR: How young?
STUDENT: Uh, I believe he was 16.
PROFESSOR: You believe?
STUDENT: No. He was definitely 16. His birthday was . . .
PROFESSOR: That's fine. Please continue.
STUDENT: This young man bought a motorcycle. It was a Honda 350 . . .

PROFESSOR: Is that all he did?

STUDENT: Pardon?

PROFESSOR: When he bought this cycle, did he do anything else?

STUDENT: He bought a helmet, he bought a rear-view mirror, he . . .

PROFESSOR: How would you, as a lawyer, Ms. Jones, characterize *what* this young man did at the dealership?

STUDENT: Oh, he made a contract. He entered into a contract.

PROFESSOR: Continue.

STUDENT: This young man entered a contract to buy a motorcycle and took delivery. He only paid a part of the price—a down payment. After two weeks, he decided he didn't want the motorcycle any more. He had gotten engaged and his fiancée wanted a ring . . .

PROFESSOR: Really? What kind of ring?

STUDENT: Oh. Well, I don't know.

PROFESSOR: Nor should you. It's irrelevant. So is the reason he didn't want the motorcycle anymore. Extract only the vital facts from these decisions, Ms. Jones.

STUDENT: Yes, sir. He told the dealer to pick up the motorcycle and he refused to pay the balance due. The dealer sued him for this money. The court said . . .

PROFESSOR: *Sued* him, Ms. Jones? *Sued* this poor young man? The dealer had his motorcycle back. Why was the dealer upset?

STUDENT: Well, uhn . . .

PROFESSOR: What had the young man done that was so wrong?

STUDENT: I guess the dealer was going to lose his profit.

PROFESSOR: That's true, Ms. Jones. But, again as a lawyer, how would you characterize what the boy did?

STUDENT: Oh. He breached the contract.

PROFESSOR: Very good. He *breached* the contract. Please continue with this dramatic saga.

STUDENT: The court ruled in favor of the boy. It said that he was an infant and . . .

PROFESSOR: An *infant*? You said he was 16.

STUDENT: The law defines anyone under the age of majority as an infant.

PROFESSOR: And what is the age of majority?

STUDENT: I'm not exactly sure, but 16 is in there.

PROFESSOR: Sixteen is in there somewhere, hm?

STUDENT: That's right. Well, the court said that since he was an infant, he could avoid the contract.

PROFESSOR: Get off scot free?

STUDENT: That's right.

PROFESSOR: Hardly seems fair, does it? Our 16-year-old infant can break a contract with impunity, but a 19-year-old adult can't.

STUDENT: The court said this was a public policy decision. You have to draw the line somewhere. I mean, you can't very well hold a four-year-old to a contract to pay $100 a month.

PROFESSOR: In other words, a dealer who sells a motorcycle to a four-year-old deserves what he gets?

STUDENT: Uhm. I'm not sure if that's what I mean or not.

PROFESSOR: Before we get to public policy, let's return to the question at hand. How would you describe the contract in this case?

STUDENT: Not worth the paper it's written on?

PROFESSOR: Please leave the humor, such as it is, in this class to me, Ms. Jones.

STUDENT: It's a voidable contract.

PROFESSOR: Voidable. Yes, it is a voidable contract. Now Ms. Jones, you are representing this motorcycle dealer. Not a bright fellow, really. After all, he's sold motorcycles to four-year-olds, right? But even fools deserve good lawyers and you've agreed to take the case. You dig up some facts about this 16-year-old contract-breaker. For one thing, he lives 50 miles outside of Salt Lake City and works in the city itself. Commutes every day. He's also an orphan. Does this give you any ideas?

STUDENT: Sure. I'd argue that the motorcycle was a *necessary*. It's a rule in the majority of states that an infant can't break a contract he enters to buy necessaries—transportation to and from his job, for instance.

PROFESSOR: Very good. Now let's change the facts. Let's take your four-year-old. We'll assume his feet don't reach the pedals on a Harley-Davidson, so let's say he buys a tricycle, on time. The same situation.

STUDENT: Does he pedal to Salt Lake City every day?

There you have a typical, if fanciful, example of a Socratic session. Forget the legal principles; get the flavor of the game. Note that the entire exchange could be summarized by a professor in a lecture as: "Contracts of infants, who are defined by the law as anyone under the age of majority, are voidable by the child. The exception is a contract for 'necessaries,' that is, what the child needs for daily survival."

Some professors who use the Socratic system get carried

away and engage in a little verbal whipping, especially if they feel you haven't done the homework. But take it in stride. Every lawyer in the country has survived the Socratic method of teaching; you will too. Remember too that because the classes are so large, you will not be called on often.

Here's a trick I used frequently: The best way to beat the nervousness in Socratic sessions is to volunteer when you know the answer. This relieves the tension and if you do it frequently enough, you may, depending on your school's grading practices, be able to earn extra credit.

Often professors modify the traditional case approach to instruction. Rather than grilling students, they use assigned cases as points of departure for class discussions in which everyone is encouraged to participate. I found this to be the classroom environment most conducive to learning. It avoids both the tedium of pure lecture and the consuming uneasiness that sometimes accompanies Socratic classes.

ASSIGNMENTS

Your assignments will be almost exclusively from "casebooks," which are somber-looking tomes that include actual court decisions (or excerpts from them), each one representing a rule of law.

It is these cases that you will "brief," or synopsize, to aid in your recitation in class and in your comprehension of the rule of law each case represents. (Chapter 6 illustrates what these decisions look like and how to brief them.)

In addition to cases, you will usually be expected to read short discussions of the cases (which appear after each case) written by the author or editor of the casebook. These blurbs, or "notes" as they are called, are quite helpful in understanding recalcitrant cases and for summarizing and reconciling several seemingly inconsistent decisions.

You can expect assignments to be long: 100 pages per week in a single class is not unheard of. The average per class is usually between 40 and 60 pages per week. Don't fall behind in the reading. It is extremely difficult to get caught up once you fail to complete assignments; even if you sincerely intend to get to the unread portion of the assignment later in the semester, you probably won't have time to do so.

A word of warning: Assignments will usually be posted before your first class session; ferret them out and do them. Professors have been known to call on students on the first day, even before they have cracked open their brand-new notebooks.

GRADES AND EXAMS

Because class rank is so important to potential employers and for determining such honors as invitations to join the law review, few law schools offer a pass-fail arrangement. Most grade their students by numbers (60 through 100) or the traditional letter standing (F through A). Grading is anonymous at many schools. You will be given a code number around exam time, which will be known only to you and a computer; professors don't know whose blue book they're grading, and other students won't know what grade you received when marks are posted.

First-year grades are based exclusively on one or two written exams (the technique for preparing for and taking these tests is discussed at great length later in this book). The one exception to this is your legal research and writing class, in which you'll be graded on writing projects and an oral presentation.

What are these exams like? Although some professors use multiple-choice and true-false exams, the majority of law school exams are essay tests. You will be give a fact pattern full of all sorts of nasty things—murders, car accidents, breached contracts, kidnappings. You'll be astonished at how much trouble people can get themselves into in the space of one paragraph.

And who gets them out of trouble?

You, of course. The question will ask: "You be the judge. What is the outcome of the case?" Or perhaps: "You are counsel for X. What arguments would you make on his behalf?"

After a period of analysis and outlining, you'll write the answer in a blue book. Then you go home, having survived the fastest three hours of your life, and wait three months to find out your grade (law school tests patience, as well as endurance).

Occasionally some professors will give you credit for class performance, perhaps as much as 10 percent of the final grade, based on your skills in recitation and willingness to volunteer. Some make this extra credit; a few professors will subtract points if you're unprepared (although I have never heard of a professor who penalized students who had done the assignment but who reached an incorrect conclusion or were simply unable to understand the point of a case).

FIRST-YEAR COURSES

You may be curious about the courses you'll be taking your first year.[1] In most schools these are year-long courses, and they will occupy two or three hours a week of lecture time during both semesters. The contents of each course are described briefly in this section. In addition, I have included the basic headings of my course outlines under each topic to show you specifically what topics are usually covered. (Bear in mind, though, that professors often adjust curricula to reflect both their own interests and current trends they see as important; your course content will probably vary somewhat.)

Civil Procedure

In the course on civil procedure you will learn procedural law, which is the body of rules that regulate how people sue one another for civil wrongs (as opposed to the "substantive" law, which describes what rights they have in general and when they will be permitted to enforce those rights). In short, this course will teach you how a civil (not criminal) lawsuit works.

[1] Those of you already into your first year or beyond and those of you wondering about what courses you should take during your second and third years, refer to Chapter 14.

The procedural law that you will study in this course will be federal civil procedure, not state. You learn federal law primarily because: (1) you have to learn it sooner or later; and (2) federal procedural law is particularly streamlined and obviously much more uniform than the laws of the various states.

In some schools, there may be a second- or third-year course dealing with the civil procedure laws of that state in which the school is located or a state in which prospective graduates will seek employment (such as New York or California). The state course is optional, however, and usually is taken solely for the purposes of preparing for the bar exam.

    I. Jurisdiction
       A. Of the courts
       B. Over the parties
       C. Venue and change of venue
   II. Statute of limitations
  III. The complaint
  IV. The answer
   V. Counterclaim
  VI. Third-party practice
 VII. Motion practice
VIII. Provisional remedies
  IX. The trial
   X. Judgment
  XI. Appeals
 XII. Res judicata—former trials

Constitutional Law

It may help to refer to Appendix One before looking over this course discussion because the role of the Constitution in American law is discussed there. Basically, this pivotal document establishes the essential governmental framework and the rights of individuals. This course is the study of these legal concepts, taught primarily through decisions of the Supreme Court, the final arbiter on constitutional issues.

The major subjects you will learn are the Supreme Court's

authority to declare congressional acts unconstitutional, the legal relationships between state governments and the federal government and among the branches of federal government (the courts, Congress, and the president), the powers exercised by the federal government, and the protections afforded individuals. You may also learn something about the mechanics of Supreme Court practice.

    I. Role of the courts in constitutional issues
   II. Relation between federal and state governments
      A. The Commerce Clause
      B. Taxing, spending, military, foreign affairs
  III. State regulation of economic matters
  IV. Immunities and interstate relationships
   V. Separation of powers among the three branches
     of government
  VI. Civil rights of individuals—The Bill of Rights
 VII. Due process
VIII. Equal protection under the laws
  IX. First Amendment—freedom of expression
   X. First Amendment—religion
  XI. Constitutional litigation

Contracts

The concept of the contract, an agreement that can be enforced in court, is so central to our daily personal and professional lives that it is perhaps the most important course in first-year law school. Throughout your legal schooling and your practice, you will continually refer to the material you are taught during the two semesters of contracts class.

Contracts appear literally in every area of law you might practice. Their application to real estate transactions and corporate law is obvious. Contracts also play a large role in tort law and divorce law—through the use of settlement agreements to resolve disputes without going to court—as well as in antitrust law, trust and estate law, taxation, and even some types of criminal law.

Yet even if your speciality doesn't directly involve much

contract work, you're sure to receive calls from relatives who've just found that their Florida dream condo is actually an acre of pungent Dade County swamp and who are begging you to find a loophole in their contract.

The course will teach you who can make a contract, what rules must be complied with in order for a contract to be enforceable in court, how the obligations created by a contract arise and are then discharged, and what defenses exist in suits based on contracts. You'll also learn of certain special contractual situations, such as the rules relating to contracts made for the benefit of other people and transfers of rights under a contract.

    I. Making a contract
       A. Offer
       B. Acceptance
       C. Parol evidence rule
       D. Consideration
       E. Promissory estoppel
       F. Capacity of the parties to contract
    II. Avoiding or reforming contracts
   III. Breach of contract
   IV. Damages for breach
    V. Restitution
   VI. Specific performance
  VII. Third-party beneficiaries
 VIII. Assignment of contracts
   IX. Statute of frauds
    X. Discharge of contracts
   XI. Illegal contracts

Criminal Law

The course on criminal law will teach you the *substantive* law of crimes (what murder *is*, for instance), not the law of *procedure* in criminal actions (how to *try* someone for murder). This subject is the one you'll probably be the most familiar with going into law school, thanks to television, movies, and novels.

In the crimes course, you will learn the elements to be proved by the prosecuting attorney in order to allow a jury to find a person guilty of a crime, defenses, constitutional requirements for protecting the rights of the accused, and miscellaneous aspects of criminal law, such as statutory construction, sentencing, and social policies to be served by criminal law.

The subject is a fascinating one in itself whether your interest is defense or prosecution. Those of you planning careers in corporate firms, though, shouldn't think you'll never have to deal with criminal law. Often, even in the prestige firms, litigation attorneys have learned their craft as U.S. or state's attorneys, prosecuting criminal cases. Moreover, it's not unusual for corporate clients to get themselves into situations in which it is alleged they have committed some type of white-collar crime.

    I. Criminal law generally
        A. Mens rea—culpable state of mind
        B. Ignorance, mistake, intoxication
        C. Parties to crimes—accessories, etc.
        D. Defenses to crimes
            1. Infancy
            2. Mental defect
            3. Justification
            4. Duress
            5. Entrapment
            6. Renunciation
   II. Specific crimes
        A. Solicitation, conspiracy, attempt, facilitation
        B. Assault, menacing, reckless endangerment
        C. Homicide
        D. Sex offenses
        E. Kidnapping, unlawful imprisonment, coercion
        F. Criminal trespass and burglary
        G. Criminal mischief
        H. Arson
         I. Larceny and robbery
        J. Fraud, bribery, and business crimes

        K. Drug offenses
        L. Offenses against public sensibilities
    III. Sentencing and punishment
        A. Philosophy behind
        B. Classifications of offenses
        C. Types of sentences

Legal Research and Writing

The course on research and writing will teach you the techniques for researching legal issues. It also will give you some experience in preparing the types of documents attorneys work with every day. You will learn what types of legal books and journals exist, how to use them, where to find them, what computers can do for you, what legal services exist and how to use their publications.

The course will familiarize you with the place that will be your home away from home for the rest of your professional life: the law library. You will be given short quizzes or projects, in which you must track down information in a kind of legal treasure hunt.

During the first part of the course (and usually no longer than four to six weeks), you will learn about the sources of the law and where to find them. After that, most schools will have you use these tools to complete two writing projects: (1) a memorandum of law; and (2) a court brief.

The memorandum of law will be the major project of your first semester. In law firm practice, memoranda are the essential means of communicating with other attorneys in the firm and with clients. A memorandum is a lawyer's response to a legal question. "If I haven't signed the contract yet, can I get out of it?" "The driver I ran into was drunk and speeding. Am I still liable to him?" When presented with one of these questions—either from the attorney you're working for, or from a client directly—your task is to write a memorandum of law that states the facts, the rules of law that you believe would apply to those facts, and then the conclusion.

In preparing the memorandum for your course, you will be given a hypothetical fact pattern and a related legal question. A simple example is this:

John Jones was driving his car late at night when he fell asleep at the wheel. Going 40 mph, the car broke through a barricade that was designed to withstand direct impact of vehicles going 70. The car tumbled down an embankment and struck a propane tank, knocking the tank into a nearby mobile home and setting it on fire. The occupant of the mobile home, Sam Smith, was seriously injured. Mr. Jones is uninsured and bankrupt. Mr. Smith has come to your firm asking if he will succeed in a suit against the maker of the highway barricade. Please write a memorandum of law stating whether or not such a suit will be successful.

In the second semester, your project will be a continuation of your memorandum. You will write an "appellate brief"—not to be confused with a "case brief," which you'll recall is a synopsis of a court decision. An appellate brief is a long document written by the parties to a trial after the trial is over. The brief arises when the loser at the trial complains that the trial court decision was incorrect. The brief is addressed to an appellate court (a court that does not hear trials but whose primary purpose is to correct mistakes made in the trial court). The brief states, in a very stylized format, why the trial court decision was wrong and why the appellate court should overturn that decision. Of course, the other side will write its own brief stating why the trial court was right.

After submitting their appellate briefs to the court, the lawyers for each side have an opportunity to stand up before the judges of the appellate court and present oral arguments, summarizing their major points in the brief. Similarly, the high point of the second semester is an actual oral argument, called a "moot court," in which you will appear before professors or senior students sitting as "judges" and argue the position you have taken.

An appellate brief assignment based on the above memorandum might look something like this:

You have just been notified that a verdict has been rendered in the case of Smith *v.* Fred's Highway Barricade Company. *The jury found in favor of the barricade company. Your client, Sam Smith, wishes to appeal this decision to the court of appeals. Attached are relevant portions of the trial*

*transcript. Please prepare an appellate brief setting forth all
legal arguments why the trial court was in error and why a
verdict should be entered in favor of Mr. Smith, or in the
alternative, a new trial should be ordered.*

I include below the course outline, as I have for all of the
first-year course. You should note, however, that this outline is
also a helpful list of sources where you will find the law; you
might wish to mark it for future reference.

    I. Court reporters
        A. Federal decisions
        B. State decisions
    II. Digests and summaries of decisions
   III. Annotated law reports
   IV. Constitutional and legislative law
        A. Constitutions
        B. Federal legislation
        C. State legislation
        D. Municipal legislation
        E. Legislative history
    V. Administrative law
        A. Federal
        B. State
   VI. Restatements of the law and uniform state laws
  VII. Shepardizing and updating
 VIII. Secondary materials
        A. Looseleaf services
        B. Legal encyclopedias
        C. Periodicals
        D. Treatises
   IX. Other materials
    X. Use of computers in legal research
   XI. Foreign country legal research

Real Property

The real property course will take you back into the cob-
webbed halls of the ancient common law as it existed in England when ownership of land was synonymous with power.

The law developed special rules—complex and arcane—to regulate the ownership, use, and transfer of land.

Today, although most of the stodgy accoutrements of the old-time law of real property have been discarded, many old rules remain, modified by modern statutes and court decisions.

Specifically, you will work your way through the concept of possession of land and objects; the types of rights (called "interests") one can have in real property; the legal nature of the landlord-tenant relationship; the methods by which one can transfer property and protect the parties' interests in the process; newer forms of real estate ownership (co-ops and condos); and the public and private regulation of land use.

Real property courses tend to be more eclectic than others, and your professor may present other concepts in addition to, or in place of, the standard curriculum discussed here.

    I. Estates and future interests of land
   II. Adverse possession
  III. Personal property
     A. Gifts
     B. Bailment
     C. Bona fide purchasers
  IV. Landlord-tenant law
     A. Landlord's duties
     B. Tenant's duties
   V. Conveyancing
     A. Deeds
     B. Covenants of title
     C. Recording and priorities
     D. Mortgages and financing
  VI. Land use controls
     A. Covenants
     B. Easements and licenses
     C. Zoning
     D. Co-ops and condominiums

Torts

The word "tort" comes from the Latin verb meaning "to twist," as in a screw, as in somebody screwed up. A tort is a wrong for which the law provides a *civil* penalty (as opposed to a criminal one) and that isn't a breach of contract.

A car accident, a plane crash, a slip-and-fall in a building lobby, exploding soda bottles, asbestosis, a careless surgical operation, calling someone a thief when he isn't one, stealing someone's car—these are all torts. (Note that some of them also are crimes.)

In your torts class, you'll learn about "intentional" torts: hitting your neighbor (a battery), scaring your neighbor by almost hitting him (assault), locking him in a closet (false imprisonment), falsely telling him that his beloved pet turtle has died (intentional infliction of emotional distress).

You'll learn about negligence: when the law imposes liability because of carelessness (as opposed to purposeful conduct) and the defenses to it.

Products liability, a fascinating body of law that combines a number of theories and legal philosophies to protect consumers, will undoubtedly be on your professor's agenda.

You'll also learn the law of defamation (libel and slander), misrepresentation, invasion of privacy, and other less common torts.

    I. Intentional torts
      A. Battery
      B. Assault
      C. False imprisonment
      D. Mental distress
      E. Trespass—land and personal property
      F. Conversion
   II. Defenses to intentional torts
  III. Negligence
      A. Duty
      B. Causation
      C. Breach
      D. Damages
  IV. Defenses to negligence
   V. Strict liability—generally
  VI. Strict liability—defective products
 VII. Misrepresentation

VIII. Slander and libel
  IX. Privacy
   X. Harm to financial relationships
  XI. Wrongful use of legal process

VARIATIONS

Although the above-mentioned courses are those most frequently required of students, you may find your school offers a different arrangement of courses, or even different courses altogether.

For instance, New York University Law School offers, instead of the traditional legal writing and research, an interesting course called Lawyering—a six-credit program that includes instruction in drafting skills, research, client interviewing and counseling, case analysis, and problem handling. There is also an opportunity to work out scenarios encountered in the real legal world through role playing.

For students in the evening division of their law school (generally a four-year program), the required first-year courses are spread out over their first and second year.

Most schools also require you to take an ethics course and your school will probably have a few upper-class requirements, such as corporations or wills. (See Chapter 14 for a discussion of upper-class courses you might wish to take.)

Chapter Five

⚖ Daily Survival in the Classroom

The preceding chapter discussed what to expect in class. It's now time to delve into the mechanics of the LCM system as they relate to classroom work. We'll look at several things: what study aids are available, how to handle daily classwork, and the study group. First of all—how to read.

READING IN LAW SCHOOL

Speed Reading

You may know how to read. Or you may think you do. I thought I did, too, especially since I'd been a professional writer before going to law school.

I was surprised.

One week into my first semester, the volume of material I was assigned—about 300 pages a week—was too much for my reading habits. I started to fall behind; then I tried speeding through the assignments to catch up. That was pointless; I comprehended nothing.

I suddenly realized I needed some help and asked advice from friends I knew could read rapidly. Their suggestions helped me immensely, practically doubling my reading speed; I present these tips here.

Essentially, the technique I used is this: You mentally divide each line of printed material into two or three segments and then train your eye to pause in the middle of each imaginary segment of the line and only there. For instance:

> Contrary to the defendant's depiction of the reasons for the hostility between the plaintiff and the four representatives of the buyer, the evidence produced has clearly shown . . .

↑   ↑   ↑

pause   pause   pause

The reasoning behind this technique is that reading speed is correlated to eye movement. Therefore, the fewer times the eye pauses per line, the faster the line will be read. In terms of comprehension, too, this method is supposedly more efficient than word-by-word reading because the stream of the author's thoughts will flow into your mind undisrupted by random stoppages or jumps of your eye around the page.

As you become accustomed to this method of speed reading, which requires practice, you will be able to decrease the number of stops per line from three to perhaps two or even one on short lines.

Vocabulary

One problem hampering your reading at first will be the unfamiliarity with legal vocabulary. It takes time to get to know what the legal terms mean. Normal people don't say, "assumpsit" or "a fortiori" at cocktail parties—at least not if they want to be invited back. Buy a paperback (not hardcover) legal dictionary and keep it with you at all times as you study during the first semester.

Other Reading Tips

Your understanding of the material you are assigned will be dramatically increased if you read it twice. Yes, this sounds burdensome, but try the experiment yourself: Take an unfamiliar passage and see if two readings don't dramatically improve your comprehension. While textbooks and law review articles don't always require such double duty if written in straightforward style, case decisions—the bulk of your class assignments—*must* be read twice, at least during your first semester.

Marking important text is a personal matter. I found underlining wasn't helpful to me. It slowed my reading and I found that the act of underlining often replaced the process of my learning the material (there is always that sense of "I'll mark it now and go back and learn it later"). When I found the important parts of cases in my assignments, I would read them once. I then circled the entire passage or bracketed it with a vertical line in the margin.

Unless a passage is so clearly important that it sets off bells and whistles on the first reading, postpone any such marking until your second time through the material. When you're not familiar with the subject, you tend to mark everything you read, which obviously undermines the whole point of highlighting text.[1]

A GUIDE TO BOOKS AND STUDY AIDS

The preceding section told you *how* to read. This section will tell you *what* you're going to read—what books you'll be required to buy and from which you'll do your class assignments and what optional materials you may wish to read to help you in your studies.

Casebooks

Casebooks, which you will be required to buy for class, contain edited court decisions, or cases. Reading from these

---

[1] Hello. I'm a footnote. Since this is the section on reading, it seemed like an appropriate place to introduce myself. You may have met some of my distant cousins in undergraduate school: they were those gray blobs at the bottom of the page—blobs that you weren't assigned and wouldn't have read if they had been. Well, in law school, we footnotes have come into our own. Hundreds of us lurk in your future, and you can't afford to ignore us anymore. Remember that if a judge or author has something vital to say, something that should be prominent and lit up with a neon sign, something your professor is sure to grill you on in class, it might very well be found buried in one of us.

books will comprise the bulk of your assignments. These books will also have, interspersed between the cases, sections called "notes" (or something similar), in which the author gives you additional information about the case itself or the legal topic it deals with.

Law is a dynamic field, and casebooks must be updated to incorporate new decisions. In addition to the hardcover casebook, you will often be required to buy a paperback supplement, which includes recent decisions and legislative changes that have occurred since the hardcover edition of the book came out. Warning: *Do not neglect to read the supplements*. Since they reflect the up-to-the-minute state of the law, professors often put greater emphasis on the cases in the supplement than they do on older cases.

While you may be tempted to sell your casebook after the course is finished, remember that they remain valuable for years as sources for cases and as bibliographies about the topic of law they cover. Even in practice, although you would rarely cite a casebook in a court brief, you might very likely refer to one of your old casebooks for lists of relevant treatises and articles that you *could* cite, or to help you begin research into a subject of law you need some refreshing in.

Treatises

Treatises are lengthy multivolume works that exhaustively discuss in narrative form an area of law. They do not reprint cases, but provide synopses of important ones and include detailed information on the history of the legal subject, what legislative changes have occurred, what the philosophy behind the law is, and so on.

The classic examples are Williston's and Corbin's treatises on contracts, both of which you will become familiar with before too long.

You don't buy treatises for your personal use (not only because of the expense; who wants to lug around a twenty-two-volume set of books?). In fact, treatises often are not helpful for students since they include so much detailed information (they are intended primarily for practicing attorneys and judges). Still, if you're stumped by a difficult question, you'll almost certainly find the answer in the treatise dealing with the topic although you may have to do a little digging to find it.

Hornbooks

A hornbook is a minitreatise, also called a textbook, and is intended primarily for students. Like a treatise, it does not contain the text of court decisions but rather presents a straightforward discussion of the law. A hornbook will say, "The rule of law is . . . ," whereas a casebook will present a sample case that contains a version of that rule. Perhaps the most famous hornbook, and one of the best ever written, is *Prosser on Torts*. If you're near a law book store or library, stop in and ask to see a copy to get an idea of what a hornbook is.

Hornbooks are usually hardcovers, but they are affordable. They're an excellent investment, especially around exam time when the library copies will invariably be checked out. Although they are intended mostly for students, you will use them in your practice. A good resource is the popular line of paperback hornbooks called the Nutshell series, which gives brief overviews of most areas of law.

Legal Outlines

Legal outlines are commercially sold paperbound booklets designed to summarize an entire law school course, often following the organization and contents of specific casebooks. They supposedly are to be used as an aid to the casebook although many students often use them instead of the casebook (more on this later). Outlines present a synopsis of each case in the casebook and include a discussion of the rule of law the case represents and other information about the subject.

These are, as the name suggests, in outline format, and are similar to the master outline you will write using the LCM system. Some of these outlines are nearly as lengthy as the casebooks they digest. Note that some of them are merely paperbound hornbooks in outline format; they don't correspond to any particular casebook.

Case Briefs

Case briefs are nothing more than ready-briefed cases (also called "canned briefs"). Often they are in a form that allows them to be torn out of the book and inserted into your own notebooks. They, like many of the legal outlines, usually are written to correspond to specific casebooks and often offer a subscription service through which you will be sent briefs of the cases recently added to the latest editions of the casebook or its supplement.

Case briefs have some marginal value in presenting a summary of a case, but they are no substitute for reading the assigned cases and as such I would put them low on your list of potential study aids.

Law Review Articles and Periodicals

The law review is a scholarly journal published periodically, usually quarterly. Every law school has its own, and some schools have several, each dealing with a specialty such as environmental, communications, or antitrust law.

The articles in these journals are written by professors, practicing lawyers, and judges, although a portion of the space is reserved for students who contribute smaller articles. The topics of the articles are generally very esoteric and deal with the finer points of law. Often they will express authors' opinions about areas of law that they feel need to be changed.

Because they are written by experts for experts, most law review articles will not be helpful to students in their first year. Occasionally, however, a law review will present an excellent overview of an area of law and will do so with particular clarity and perception. Your professor may recommend such articles and you should read them.

You will also find dozens of legal magazines, ranging from the well-known *ABA Journal* down to limited circulation, specialized magazines. Although very little in any of these magazines will help you directly in your studies, I recommend picking up one or two that interest you and reading them at your leisure. These will give you an idea of what practical issues attorneys are currently confronting and of how attorneys manage the business aspects of their practice (hiring staff, renting space, using computers, and so on).

High-Tech Materials

Since the first edition of this book was published, there has been a virtual information revolution. Law study has, like so many other institutions and endeavors, been dramatically affected by this trend.

VIDEO AND AUDIO TAPES

It is now possible to find many of the study aids I've mentioned on both audio and video tape, giving you the benefit of seeing on screen or hearing lectures by well-known legal educators. Video tapes are particularly helpful in upper-class courses such as trial advocacy, where you will learn such things as gestures, courtroom speaking techniques, and handling witnesses. To be able to see experts orchestrate a trial on tape is a major benefit to future litigators.

Camcorders and other personal video tape machines can help you prepare for your moot court argument in your first-year legal research class. Try taping yourself and studying both your argument and your body language, voice level, and so on. Practicing in front of this all-seeing eye will also prepare you psychologically for your appearance before the "judges."

If you intend to audio tape a professor's lecture, be sure to ask permission first. I would not recommend this as a regular practice, however, because taking notes in class eliminates a lot of the "noise" and superfluous material that accompanies lectures. But if you anticipate that a lecture will deal with a particularly difficult topic, and you wish to listen to it again, a tape of the session might be helpful.

COMPUTER RESEARCH

Computers have, of course, now become standard equipment in legal study and practice. Lexis, Westlaw and Veralex are the major systems used for computerized legal research. Most trial lawyers in the country do at least part of their research with one of these systems. You will learn about these in your research and writing course.

In addition, most legal libraries have systems that streamline "cite-checking" (verifying the accuracy of references to court cases and other legal authorities)—a notoriously tedious, but vital, task for students and young attorneys. You also can take advantage of CD-ROM machines (Compact Disk—Read Only Memory), computer storage systems that contain huge amounts of legal materials on a tiny disk (identical to music CDs). The CD-ROM systems allow you to search through treatises, indexes, and other legal materials at literally the speed of light.

INTERACTIVE SYSTEMS

There is another interesting type of software on the market now—interactive programs. These allow the user with a standard personal computer to create legal documents in response to questions the computer itself asks. These interactive programs (meaning that the user and the computer can respond to each other) are not artificial intelligence systems and cannot replace an attorney's experience and judgment. But when it comes to creating customized legal documents for litigation or business transactions, many of the mechanical and repetitive aspects of assembling those materials can be left to the machine.

As a student, you will probably not have much need or opportunity to use such a system, but if you get access to one—if your library has a PC, for instance, or if you're clerking in a law firm—you should try it out. It will greatly supplement your legal education, both in the discovery of what computers can do for you and how legal documents are assembled.

Using Study Aids

Treatises, hornbooks, legal outlines, and case briefs are the major study aids available to you. How do they fit into the LCM system?

Students often buy case briefs, or canned briefs, and use them frequently. But if you use them *instead* of briefing the cases yourself, you'll be doing yourself a major disservice. For one thing, commercial briefs can miss issues. Also, they tend to be very short and may deal with complex legal issues in a superficial way.

More important, though, briefing cases is a skill that you must learn. There'll come a day when a partner sticks her head in your office and says, "Jones, I just heard about this new case, *Hansel* v. *Gretel*. Get a brief to me in a half-hour." There won't be any commercial briefs you can turn to (and even if there were, it would be malpractice to rely on it instead of the actual text of the case).

Essentially, the same rule applies with the other types of study aids: They should supplement, not replace, your briefing of cases and reading of assigned materials. There is nothing wrong with such aids but, as the underlying philosophy of the LCM system maintains, you get out of school what you put into it. If you wrestle through a case and brief it, you'll truly understand it. You'll *see* the facts. You'll have the decision with you for years. If you rely on a predigested brief or an abstract rule of law from a hornbook, you'll forget it within a week.

It is often helpful, before reading assigned cases, to read the section in a hornbook or other study aid dealing with the topic of law your class is currently covering. You will not only get a good background for the subject, but you may find that the assigned cases have themselves been discussed by the hornbook author. (A good tip: Look up assigned cases in the hornbook's "Table of Cases"; you will find that many of the cases have been included in the book.)

DAILY CLASSWORK

In this section, I'm going to tell you the technique I adopted for my classwork. You may want to use it; you may not. The important thing is to find a system that you are comfortable with and that aids in your ability to organize and locate materials when it comes time to create your outline.

The Big Three Sources

The essence of your work in law school is to gather information from three sources:

- You will brief assigned cases.
- You will take notes in class.
- You will take notes from outside reading.

I bought three spiral-bound notebooks for each class (spiral because outlining requires a lot of flipping back and forth, and I always seem to misplace loose pages). One notebook was for my case briefs; one was for class notes; the third was for notes I took from outside sources.

A word on this last category. Professors may give you outside assignments—perhaps readings from law review articles, books, or articles in nonlegal publications. In addition, if I were confused about something in class, I would often look up the subject in a hornbook or treatise and write notes on what I learned. This outside material proved to be invaluable in helping me understand concepts professors never adequately explained or sped over.

This practice of merging information from these three different sources is central to the LCM system.

Procrastination

Try to do the assigned reading and briefing as close in time as possible to the class for which it's to be covered. For instance, if in your Wednesday contracts class, you are given an assignment that's due next Wednesday, don't do the briefing until Monday or Tuesday. What?! Am I advocating procrastination? Yes. For the simple reason that the material should be fresh in your mind when discussed. Brief it too far ahead of class, and you won't be able to follow the discussion as clearly as if you'd done it the day before. And if called upon, your recitation, not to mention your composure, may suffer.

Reading assignments will be long, but it's vital that you not fall behind. If you're a week behind the professor's lectures, both what you're presently reading (last week's assignments) and what he's currently teaching (this week's assignments) will be lost on you.

Absences

Don't cut classes. All contract law is not alike. All tort law is not alike. When you take a law school course, you're not learning the absolute law, but the law according to *your* professor, who will emphasize some topics to the exclusion of others—perhaps taking an approach quite different from that taken by the legal outline you bought.

Similarly, all students are not alike. If you rely on other students' notes for classes you missed, you're gambling that they are as interested as you are in learning the material. That might not be the case.

Color Coding

Some students use unique techniques for taking notes and briefing cases—color-coded pens, for instance (I did this my first semester). As long as you don't neglect substance for technique, there's nothing wrong with doing this. If writing your torts notes in fuschia ink helps you stay organized and remember the material, by all means, go right ahead. Just be sure to buy a semester's worth of fuschia pens so you don't run out of ink just before the exam and have to drop out of the class.

Personal Computers

If you have a personal computer, use it. I often typed my notes after class. If laptop computers or PCs had been available then I would have begged, borrowed, or stolen one and used it daily. The ability to cut and paste, to merge files, to check spelling and use other word processing features will drastically cut down on the time and effort required when you create your master outline. You can create "macros"—replicating dozens of commands or words by pressing a single key—that will reproduce standardized information in your briefs.

Of particular help in the LCM system is the automatic outlining capabilities built into most word-processing systems. This feature will save hours and greatly speed the writing of your own master outlines. All you need to do is hit the return key and then tab in the desired number of spaces for your subcategories. The computer automatically prints out the proper number or letter level for the subcategories. For instance, the following outline was created entirely by my word-processing system:

I. Torts
  A. Products liability
    1. Strict liability
      a. For dangerous drugs
        (1) General rule
          (a) Restatement of torts
          (b) Caselaw
            i) *Jones* case
            ii) *Smith* case
          (c) Statutes
        (2) Minority rule
      b. For dangerous cosmetics

All I typed was the words you see. The computer itself "remembered" what level of subcategory letter or number to use. And if I have to add a new category in the middle, the computer will automatically renumber or reletter all subsequent levels.

In addition, database programs or the mini databases built into some word-processing software will greatly aid in the assembly of your outline by allowing you to search for all cases, notes, and references dealing with, say, slander and libel or for all cases handed down in New York.

THE STUDY GROUP

Law is not practiced in isolation. There is not one attorney, judge, or legal philosopher whose final product cannot be improved by comments and criticisms from others. One of your most humbling experiences as a student or new attorney will be to explain a very complicated legal rule to a layperson, only to have that listener ask a very uncomplicated, unlegal question that points out the fallacy of your reasoning. A variety of perspectives on a legal issue are immensely helpful in solving legal problems.

In law firms, attorneys always meet in conferences and engage in less formal discussions when they are attempting to adopt a litigation strategy or plan a business deal. The corresponding phenomenon in law school is the study group.

Are such groups important?

Not necessarily. Consider, for instance, what would happen if a group of attorneys sat down at a conference table to discuss an issue yet had no idea of the rules of law involved. The meeting would be a waste of time; the attorneys should get themselves into the library and do some preliminary research first.

It's the same with study groups. If you don't come to them with sufficient knowledge, they're a waste of time.

By all means, talk with other students; there's no better way to find out what you don't know (which is much more important, of course, than finding out what you *do* know). But it's probably smart to keep these get-togethers informal and short. I found it most helpful to meet with my group during the study week prior to the final exams. But I did this only after I had spent much time studying on my own for the exams. Although it can be a valuable supplement to the education process, group study is no substitute for learning the material yourself.

Chapter Six

⚖ How to Brief Cases

*[For a preview of this chapter,
see Recap 1 on p. 93.]*

As you learned earlier, your assignments for law school classes will be to read actual court decisions, which have been edited and reprinted in your casebook. You'll recall too that it is not enough simply to read these cases. You must "brief," or digest, them as well. This chapter will tell you how to do this.

THE IMPORTANCE OF BRIEFING

The process of writing case briefs, which are nothing more than synopses of court decisions,[1] does four vital things for you:

- Briefs teach you rules of law, because a decision is by definition a record of the process of applying a legal rule to a set of facts.
- Briefs familiarize you with the mechanism of how courts work (e.g., how trials are managed, what witnesses can say, which courts are more powerful than others, how evidence is used, how one complains about judges who make errors). Even if the issues the court is looking at have nothing to do

[1] A decision, by the way, is a written opinion by the court in which it decides who at a trial—the plaintiff or the defendant—should win the case and why. These decisions are published in books and maintained in on-line computer systems for lawyers to use in their law practice.

with these mechanics, you will learn a great deal about them simply by reading the decision.

- Briefing cases in school builds skills in a technique that all lawyers must master for their practice. These court decisions are the weapons lawyers use, and they are helpful weapons only if they are boiled down to a brief format.
- The briefing process will allow you to endure Socratic sessions. Only by having the essence of the case before you, in a brief, can you recite the case in class and respond to the professor's questions about it.

THE BASIC MECHANICS

Reading the Case

Read each case twice.[2] The first time through don't take any notes. Read it quickly and informally. Get a sense of what is going on. On the second reading, go more slowly. Take notes in the margin, circle important points (don't hesitate to mark up your books; which lawyer would *you* rather go to— one whose books were filled with notes and underlinings or one whose books looked pristine and untouched?). It is after this second reading that you'll write your brief.

Format

The format of a brief can be very individualized; there are probably as many different ways of writing an effective brief as there are students in your class. The following format is more comprehensive than some, less so than others, but it will give you everything that you need.

---

[2] You might wish to read about the case in a hornbook or other commercially available study aid, as described in the previous chapter, before you read the text of the decision itself. This too should be a fast read. Read just enough to give you an idea of what the court writing the decision is getting at and to identify important (as the lawyers say, the "relevant") information as you read the text of the decision itself.

Here are the seven elements of the brief to be used in the LCM system, each of which will be discussed in depth below.

1. Case name, court, date
2. Facts
3. Procedure
4. Issues
5. Decision
6. Rule/Analysis
7. Holding

Keeping this framework in mind, let's look at a fictitious decision (which does, however, contain a real rule of law). We'll analyze each of these seven items, and then present a sample brief.

Poole v. *Doyle's Baking*
Supreme Court of Vermont
234 N.E. 567 (1932)

Larson, J. This is an action for damages in negligence. On the morning of June 10, a truck driver for Defendant Doyle's Baking Company was delivering bread to various retail locations. After his last delivery he drove the truck to a filling station, where it was gassed up. Having several hours to kill before he had to return the truck to Doyle's Baking, he then proceeded on to Smithtown to visit his girlfriend.

On the way to Smithtown the driver of the truck had a sneezing fit and lost control of the vehicle. It ran off the road and struck and injured Plaintiff Poole. The driver fled the jurisdiction. Poole sued Doyle's Baking, alleging that the company, as his employer, was responsible for the negligence of their driver.

The judge at trial instructed the jury that if the accident occurred during normal business hours, then the defendant should be liable for the acts of its employee. The jury found for the plaintiff and awarded damages of $5,000.00.

The defendant has appealed.

This court finds for the defendant.

It is well settled as law in this state that under the doctrine of respondeat superior, an employer will be liable for the negligent acts of its employees if those acts occur within the scope of employment. However, it is also an exception to the rule that employers will not be found liable if the employee is on a personal errand—what the law terms a "frolic"—at the time of the accident.

Here, evidence was submitted at trial to show that the driver had finished his work for the defendant and was on a personal errand (i.e., visiting his girlfriend) when the accident happened. Accordingly, we find that the trial judge erred in his instructions to the jury. The verdict of the lower court will be reversed.

Now let's look at each element in the LCM brief.

1. CASE NAME, COURT, AND DATE

While these elements are self-explanatory, don't assume they aren't important. Dates, locations, and level of courts are vitally significant. What's law today will be overturned tomorrow, and what is the rule in one state may not be in another.

In our example: *Poole* v. *Doyle's Baking*, Sup. Ct. Vt., 1932

2. FACTS

The facts are simply the events that gave rise to the lawsuit. For instance: the car accident, the business deal that resulted in a contract, the robbery. In your brief, list the facts in chronological order. Include only the absolute minimum, only those facts that are significant. How do you know which are legally important and which are not? You probably won't know at first. You'll include too many facts. As you continue to brief cases and get a feel for the law, you will edit out what's unnecessary.

Present one fact per line. This will help you in reciting cases; most professors prefer spontaneous presentations rather than reading. In our *Poole* case:

FACTS:

- *Plaintiff pedestrian hit by truck.*
- *Truck driver was defendant's employee.*
- *Driver had been working for defendant.*
- *On personal business when accident happened (visiting girlfriend).*

We should digress for a moment to look at how the courts refer to the parties in a lawsuit. Frequently, judges do not call them "plaintiff" and "defendant." Rather, they say, "appellant" (the one who is appealing, i.e., the loser in the trial court, who might, of course, be either the plaintiff or defendant) and "appellee" (the winner in the trial court). Since most of the decisions you read will be appellate and not trial court decisions, as I'll explain in a moment, this terminology is more convenient for the judges, who need to know which party is seeking the appeal and which party is opposing it.

Thus, be on guard that the parties in your cases may be wearing different hats. You should identify them both ways— "Plaintiff/Appellant" and "Defendant/Appellee." Or use abbreviations: "Pl/A'nt" and "D/A'ee." Many students and professors use the Greek letter π (pi) to represent the plaintiff and the letter Δ (delta) to represent the defendant.[3]

3. PROCEDURE

The facts present the activities surrounding a case up until the time of the lawsuit. Once the plaintiff walks into court for

---

[3] Be alert, too, to the fact that the parties named in the case (i.e., *Poole* v. *Doyle's Baking*) may appear in different order, depending on which court is rendering the decision. For instance, in the trial court, the plaintiff will always be named first. In the appellate courts of some states and in the U.S. Supreme Court, the first party named will be the appellant, the one doing the appealing. As if this were not confusing enough, you might even come across some old cases in which the appellant is called the "plaintiff-in-error," meaning that he is the party instituting the appeal, irrespective of whether he was the plaintiff or defendant below. Obviously, the appellee would be called the defendant-in-error—bearing witness to the fact that although the law is often perverse, it is at least symmetrical.

the first time, the procedure section of your brief begins. This section will list each step in the *legal*, as opposed to *factual*, history of the case. As you will probably be reciting these stages in class out loud, you should write them out in the same one-step-per-line format you used in the facts section.

PROCEDURE:

- *Pl/A'ee sues D/A'nt for personal injury.*
- *Trial court judge instructs jury that if accident occurred during normal business hours, then D/A'nt should be liable.*
- *Verdict for Pl/A'ee. Damages = $5,000.*
- *D/A'nt appealed.*

In nearly all of your briefs, the procedural section will lead up to the appeal. If you're not familiar with the concept of appeals, I'm going to offer a short explanation here (for more details, see Appendix One). An appeal is the process whereby the loser at trial goes to a higher court and asks that court to change the verdict, claiming that something went wrong in the court below. In our example, the baking company is claiming that the trial judge gave wrong information to the jury. Other examples of error would be allowing improper evidence into the case, not having the right number of jurors, or prejudicial testimony.

The appellate court then examines the transcript of the trial and lets the appellant tell why he thinks there was a mistake and the appellee tell why there wasn't. That court then decides and publishes its decision.

Ninety-nine percent of the cases you read in school will be appellate court decisions. Why? For one thing, trial court judges are essentially referees rather than creators and expounders of judicial opinions. Also, appellate courts have more authority than trial courts. Their decisions command more attention among lawyers and other judges.

Your procedure section ends with the appeal—the claim by the loser that some error occurred in the trial court and the plea to the appellate court to remedy it.

4. ISSUE

The issue is simply the legal question the appellate court is being asked to answer. In our example:

ISSUE:

- *Under Vermont law, is an employer liable for the negligence of its employee during business hours, even if that employee is engaged in personal business when the negligence occurs?*

If you look at this question closely, you can see that there really are two issues. Although the above question is perfectly fine as a statement of the issue, it is less cumbersome to break the sentence down like this:

ISSUE:

1. *Generally, under Vermont law, is an employer liable for the negligence of its employees during business hours?*
2. *If so, does such liability still exist if the employee is on a personal errand when the accident occurs?*

These two-issue cases are very common choices for case-book editors because a single court decision can be used to teach both the general rule and an exception to that rule.[4]

5. DECISION

The decision portion of your brief will be quite short. It indicates which of the parties the appellate court has ruled in

---

[4] Don't be confused if the court phrases the issue in a procedural way. For instance, another way of stating the issue in our *Poole* decision is to say: "Was the trial judge in error by instructing the jury that an employer is liable for the negligence of its employees even if the employee was on a personal errand at the time the negligence occurred?" The specific mistake the baking company's lawyer was pointing his finger at in our case was the way the judge told the jury what the law was. In your torts class, however, you aren't really concerned about the mechanics by which a judge instructs the jury (which you'll learn in your upper-class courses); your concern is to learn the substantive rule of law: When is an employer going to take the heat for its employees' mistakes?

favor of and what the court has decreed should happen next—
the "disposition" of the case, as it is called.

DECISION:

- *For D/A'nt, verdict reversed.*

Appellate courts have broad powers to change the decisions
rendered in the trial courts. The appellate court might say
that the trial judge was completely wrong and reverse the
entire decision below. Or the court might let stand certain
portions of the lower court's holding while reversing other
portions that it finds erroneous (this is because the appealing
party often claims that a number of mistakes were made by
the trial court). The appellate court might also "remand" the
case, that is, send it back to the lower court with instructions
to litigate the case again, this time ordering the trial judge to
instruct the jury differently.

Another option of the appellate court is to modify the decision below, neither wholly affirming nor reversing, but altering the outcome in some other way. For instance, had the
facts been different in our decision, the Vermont high court
might have held that the baking company was indeed liable
but the damages were far too high for the plaintiff's injury. It
would thus have affirmed the finding of liability but reversed
on the issue of damages.

6. RULE/ANALYSIS

This section is the most important one in the brief. It con-
sists of three parts:

- the rule of law
- the application of that rule to the facts
- the conclusion to be drawn from the logical reasoning process

The rule is a paraphrase of the principle the court has
selected from a statute or from a prior decision. (In rare cases,
if the issue has never been dealt with by the courts or legisla-

tures before, the court may create an entirely new rule of law.[5])

Following the rule of law is a short statement applying that rule to the relevant facts, and then the conclusion:

RULE/ANALYSIS:

Under the doctrine of respondeat superior, an employer will be liable for the negligent acts of its employees if those acts occur within the scope of employment. However, there's an exception to the rule: Employers will not be found liable if the employee is on a personal errand—what is called a "frolic"—at the time of the accident.

Here, the driver was on a frolic. He was therefore acting outside the scope of his employment and the D/A'nt baking company should not be liable for his negligence.

7. HOLDING

The holding is a fusion of the facts and the rule of law—and often it's quite a mouthful.

HOLDING:

When a delivery man, who has completed his rounds and is en route to visit his girlfriend during working hours negligently injures someone, the man's employer will not be liable for his employee's negligence under the exception to the rule of respondeat superior, which holds that employers will not be liable for the frolics of their employees.

[5] Beware, however: The court will be saying many things that appear to be rules and are not. For instance, judges may state what they think the rule *ought* to be. Or they might state what are indeed proper rules of law but are simply not applicable to the case before the court. Such legal musings are called "dicta," and although they are of some supportive value, they do not represent the important and controlling rule of the decision you are studying.

Let's look at *Poole* for a moment. The court might well have said, "Of course, had the owner of Doyle's Baking been riding in the truck and given the driver permission to visit his girlfriend, the law would hold the company liable." Well, that's nice to know and vaguely interesting. But it isn't the rule of law deciding the case because the owner *wasn't* in the truck and he *didn't* give his permission. The statement by the court was thus dicta.

Why so specific? In the practice of law, it is vitally important to delineate the exact precedential value of a case (when the case can be cited as support for a subsequent case). This can be done only by examining the facts of the decision and comparing them to the facts in the case an attorney is presented with. For instance, if you represented a woman injured by a delivery man who was *on* company business, would you cite *Poole* v. *Doyle's Baking* to the court as support for your claim of liability against the driver's employer? After all, the court stated clearly that employers are liable for acts of employees within the scope of employment. No, you couldn't! It was the *exception* to that rule that decided the *Poole* case. All the *Poole* case ultimately stands for is the proposition that an employer *won't* be liable under circumstances identical to those described in the fact section. It is verbose holdings like this one that let attorneys know exactly what the case represents and how strong a weapon it can be.

For you as a student, the holding is important primarily as a summary of the case and, therefore, optional unless your professor indicates that you must recite holdings. It's always a good idea to write holdings, though, at least during your first year in school. It cements the case in your mind and will make outlining much easier. A typical holding should begin with "Where" or "When" (the adverbial clause will help you fit all the necessary information into a single sentence).

Let's put all the elements together and see what our brief looks like:

POOLE V. *DOYLE'S BAKING*, SUP. CT. VT., 1932
FACTS:

- *Plaintiff pedestrian hit by truck.*
- *Truck driver was defendant's employee.*
- *Driver had been working for defendant.*
- *On personal business when accident happened (visiting girlfriend).*

PROCEDURE:

- *Pl/A'ee sues D/A'nt for personal injury.*
- *Trial court judge instructs jury that if accident occurred*

during normal business hours, then D/A'nt should be liable.

- *Verdict for Pl/A'ee. Damages = $5,000.*
- *D/A'nt appealed.*

ISSUE:

1. *Generally, under Vermont law, is an employer liable for the negligence of its employees during business hours?*
2. *If so, does such liability still exist if the employee is on a personal errand when the accident occurs?*

DECISION:

- *For D/A'nt, verdict reversed.*

RULE/ANALYSIS:

Under the doctrine of respondeat superior, an employer will be liable for the negligent acts of its employees if those acts occur within the scope of employment. However, there's an exception to the rule: Employers will not be found liable if the employee is on a personal errand—what is called a "frolic"—at the time of the accident.

Here, the driver was on a frolic. He was therefore acting outside the scope of his employment and the D/A'nt baking company should not be liable for his negligence.

HOLDING:

When a delivery man, who has completed his rounds and is en route to visit his girlfriend during working hours negligently injures someone, the man's employer will not be liable for his employee's negligence under the exception to the rule of respondeat superior, which holds that employers will not be liable for the frolics of their employees.

SYNTHESIZING CASES: DEALING WITH CONTRADICTION

The briefing process sometimes has a frustrating little twist to it. You brief one case and extract the rule easily enough. Not as bad as you thought it was going to be. You try another. This second case is even easier. Zip, zip, zip. . . . Facts, procedure, issue, decision, rule/analysis, holding. Piece of cake.

There's only one problem: The holding in the second case contradicts the first.

So, what gives?

Two Important Questions

The inconsistencies might be explained easily. The two essential questions you *must* ask when you are confronted with seemingly contradictory cases:

1. Were the decisions rendered in different court systems? Courts in different states are perfectly free to decide an identical issue in different ways. Court decisions in Alabama have no legal effect whatsoever on decisions in Mississippi. Similarly, federal courts in one circuit are not bound by the decisions of federal courts in other circuits. In such cases, you need not go through any elaborate analysis. Your answer: The cases are different because the courts are different and neither court had any legal right to require the other court to decide in its way.[6]

2. Were the dates of the decisions significantly different? If so, it is likely that you are being shown the evolutionary nature of the law. The early decision may represent the old common-law rule, the more recent one, the new trend. If this is the situation, you will undoubtedly find a statement by a judge in the second decision stating that the older decision

[6] This diversity of opinion among courts is quite common, and you will frequently hear of a majority rule of law and a minority rule of law. For instance, in tort law, contributory negligence (where a plaintiff was wholly barred from collecting any money from a defendant if the plaintiff was himself even slightly negligent and contributed to his own harm) was for years the majority rule (in about 35 states). The minority rule was the doctrine of comparative fault (in which the plaintiff's judgment is reduced, but not prohibited, if he is also at fault). It has been an interesting development to see the balance shift, as the comparative fault doctrine, clearly the more fair of the two, edges into the majority and the harsher contributory negligence rule is retained in fewer and fewer states.

should no longer be followed because of changes in society or because of public policy. (Often, if a court does not want to go through a public policy analysis to justify a change in the law, the judge will write: "The basis for this new rule of law is so obvious that authorities need not be cited. . . ." Those buzzwords mean, of course, that there *is* no authority and the court is making up law out of whole cloth.)

Look for Subtle Differences

But what if the seemingly inconsistent cases are rendered by the same court and within a few years of each other? When you come across a series of these cases, you will have to "synthesize" or reconcile them, meaning you will have to expand the rule of law each case stands for until it is broad enough to encompass all the seeming inconsistencies. The key to doing this is to read the cases again very carefully and look for subtle differences in the fact patterns.

On a separate sheet of paper, write the rule the first case stands for. Apply it to the second case. No, it doesn't quite fit. So you trim off some of the specifics of the first rule to make it more general. Try it again. Ah, now it fits both the cases. Apply this newly "synthesized" rule to the third case. Oops. Doesn't fit. Well, trim it some more, making it broader yet. There! At last you have a rule of law that applies to all three cases.

The Technique in Practice

Here's an illustration: The subject is torts. (Remember: torts are wrongs done by one person to another that don't involve crimes or contracts.) The topic under study is dangerous animals. You've read three cases. You line up your briefs for each, and here's what they say:

Decision No. 1, in which Person X, who owns kitten Teddy R, is held liable when Teddy sneaks next door and tears apart a neighbor's alligator-skin shoes.

Decision No. 2, in which Person Y, who owns the well-

known scrapper of a tomcat, Scarface, is held not liable when the cat lapped up the water in a neighbor's goldfish bowl (and ate Lucky, the goldfish, for dessert) after the neighbor had dropped off Lucky for fish-sitting while he, the neighbor, went on vacation.

Decision No. 3, in which Person Z, who owns a Persian show cat Ike, was held not liable when the feline streaked through a neighbor's kitchen to get a snack of milk she was leaving for him, and startled the neighbor, who dropped the milk on, and ruined, her new alligator-skin briefcase.

Your professor says, "Now, here we have three decisions from the same court, decided the same year, in which one pet owner was held liable and two were not for the acts of their pets. How do you explain these apparently contradictory decisions? How do you *synthesize* them?"

Let's get some perspective. What do we have to start with? A rule that seems to deal with an owner's liability for the acts of his cat. You try the following on for size:

One is liable for his cat's actions when the cat damages shoes, but not briefcases and fish.

Yes, this is true, but you're understandably afraid to offer this thought out loud in class. So you try again:

Owners' cats can do whatever they want to live animals, but not to animals made into accessories.

Alas, the budding lawyer in you isn't quite satisfied. You try again:

One will be liable for the acts of kittens but not full-grown cats.

This smacks of discrimination. Not very likely either. Let's go back to the facts and review the decisions again. In Decision 1, Teddy R's owner let him run loose, and the accident occurred on the neighbor's property. But in the second case, the fish owner had brought the fish bowl over to Y so that Y would fish-sit while the neighbor was on vacation. The neighbor knew full well of Scarface's appetite for fish.

So you formulate this rule, which covers the first two decisions:

A cat or kitten owner will be liable for the harm caused by the animal if the owner lets the animal run free on another's property, but not if the harm is caused on the animal owner's property to someone who knew the destructive nature of the animal.

That leaves us with Decision 3. The facts show the accident happened on the neighbor's property and Z let Ike run free, yet the neighbor was unable to recover damages from Z. Our rule doesn't seem to fit. What small fact is there that might be significant? Ah. In this case the neighbor with the briefcase fed Ike milk in her home. She therefore *invited* the offending cat onto her premises.

This then is the rule:

A cat or kitten owner will be liable for the harm caused by his or her animal if the owner lets the animal run free, but not (1) if the harm is caused on the owner's property to those who know of the destructive nature of the animal, or (2) if the harm is caused to those who willingly invite the animal onto their own property.

Synthesizing can be a lot of work but it is necessary for both law school and law practice, when you are daily confronted with seemingly contradictory cases.[7]

For a summary of the briefing process, see Recap 1 on page 93.

---

[7] By the way, don't despair if you find just as you finish synthesizing the last case a tiny footnote in your casebook that states: "In response to pressure from insurance companies, all states have not passed the Uniform Limitation on Cat Liability Act, which now regulates the subject and has rendered all of the foregoing cases moot." Such is the nature of law.

Chapter Seven

⚖ Sample Briefs

*[For a preview of this chapter,
see Recap 1 on p. 93.]*

The preceding chapter has described how to brief cases. This chapter will present three sample cases and model briefs, prepared according to the LCM system brief format.

The first case is a short, hypothetical one. Its purpose is to give you an idea of where the seven parts of the LCM brief can be recognized and how you should extract and rewrite them. The next two cases will increase in level of difficulty.

SAMPLE BRIEF FROM TORTS CLASS—ONE

Palmer v. *Dobbs*
Appellate Court of the State of Ned
36 N.E. 897 (1894)

Smith, J. This is an action for damages. Plaintiff Palmer made several purchases at a men's clothing store, including a new hat, and was walking down Broadway when Defendant Dobbs stopped him. Dobbs reportedly said to Palmer, "That's the ugliest hat I've ever seen in my life," and then repeated this comment to a number of passersby to the effect that Palmer felt ridiculed. As a result Palmer was unable to sleep at night and suffered from various and sundry other ailments.

Palmer sued Dobbs for mental anguish. The judge in-

structed the jury that if they found that the plaintiff's insomnia and ailments were a result of Dobbs' insult, they should
find for the plaintiff. This the jury did and awarded him
$100. Dobbs appealed to this court, claiming the judge's
instructions were erroneous.

We find for Dobbs and reverse the trial court's decision.

It is the law of this state that one man does not owe a duty
to another to prevent harm from minor insults. It is one of
the prices of living in society with other human beings that
individuals must bear certain hardships for which there can
be no legal redress.

Here, while Dobbs' behavior was perhaps contemptible
(evidence was presented that the hat, while garish, was not
overwhelmingly ugly), it does not rise to the level of conduct
for which the law offers redress, and the trial judge erred in
his instructions to the jury.

We note in passing that had Dobbs knocked the offending hat off Palmer's head, then Palmer would have had a
cause of action for battery. But such was not the case.

That was the decision as it would appear in your casebook.
Now let's see how you would mark the case upon your second
reading:

Palmer v. *Dobbs*
Appellate Court of the State of Ned
36 N.E. 897 (1894)

Procedure:	Smith J. This is an action for damages.
Facts:	Plaintiff Palmer made several purchases at a men's clothing store, including a new hat, and was walking down Broadway when Defendant Dobbs stopped him. Dobbs reportedly said to Palmer, "That's the ugliest hat I've ever seen in my life," and then repeated this comment to a number of passersby to the effect that Palmer felt ridiculed. As a result Palmer was unable to sleep at night

	and suffered from various and sundry other ailments.
Procedure:	Palmer sued Dobbs for mental anguish. The judge instructed the jury that if they found that the plaintiff's insomnia and ailments were a result of Dobbs' insult, they should find for the plaintiff. This the jury did and awarded
Procedure, Issue:	him $100. Dobbs appealed to this court, claiming the judge's instructions were erroneous.
Decision:	We find for Dobbs and reverse the trial court's decision.
Rule/Analysis:	It is the law of this state that one man does not owe a duty to another to prevent harm from minor insults. It is one of the prices of living in society with other human beings that individuals must bear certain hardships for which there can be no legal redress.
	Here, while Dobbs' behavior was perhaps contemptible (evidence was presented that the hat, while garish, was not overwhelmingly ugly), it does not rise to the level of conduct for which the law offers redress, and the trial judge erred in his instructions to the jury.
Dicta:	We note in passing that had Dobbs knocked the offending hat off Palmer's head, then Palmer would have had a cause of action for battery. But such was not the case.

Now, let's look at a brief of this case prepared according to the LCM system:

PALMER V. DOBBS, APP. CT. NED, 1894

FACTS:

- *Pl bought new hat.*
- *D stopped Pl on street, said: "That's the ugliest hat I've ever seen in my life."*

- *Other people laughed at Pl's hat.*
- *Pl couldn't sleep because of this, had other ailments.*

PROCEDURE:

- *Pl sued D, mental anguish.*
- *Judge instructed jury if Pl's problems were a result of D's insult, they should find for Pl.*
- *Verdict, for Pl. Awarded $100.*
- *D appealed.*

DECISION:

- *For D, verdict reversed.*

RULE/ANALYSIS:

The rule is that one man doesn't owe a duty to another to prevent harm from minor insults. Here, making fun of the Pl's hat was not the sort of conduct that the law provides redress for.

HOLDING:

When one man insults another, even resulting in insomnia and other ailments, the insulted party does not have a cause of action against the one making fun of him because the law is not meant to provide redress for wrongs of that sort.

You might have noticed the last paragraph in the case, where the judge offered some dicta, which you'll recall is a statement or observation that has no direct impact on the case (the comment is dicta in our example because Dobbs did not, in this instance, strike the plaintiff). You might wish to mark such statements, as I did in the sample case. Often professors will use dicta as springboards for class discussions.

Let's turn now to a slightly more difficult example, this one from Ned's neighboring state, Zed.

SAMPLE BRIEF FROM TORTS CLASS—TWO

Smith v. *Johnson*
Supreme Court of Zed
183 Zed 2nd 14 (1983)

Justice, J. This case is before us on appeal from a verdict in the county court, entered in favor of defendant. Plaintiff appeals.

The question presented in this negligence action is a simple one: Does the violation of a statutory duty impose an automatic finding of negligence upon a driver?

Plaintiff alleges error in the trial court's instructions to the jury regarding the standard of care to be followed by the defendant motorcyclist.

We agree with the plaintiff and so vacate the verdict and remand the case with instructions for a new trial.

On October 3, James Johnson bought a Honda 350 motorcycle. It was a used machine, and he purchased it for $1,000 cash from one Peter Dudley, who had himself purchased it new from a dealer outside the state. Johnson had previously driven a motorcycle only once—when he was overseas with the armed forces, stationed in Germany. That machine was a BMW. The controls of a BMW are similar to those of a Honda, but they are not identical.

After purchasing the motorcycle, Johnson started it and began to drive it home. Dudley stopped him and asked him if he (Johnson) wanted Dudley to drive it home for him. In that way Johnson could practice in his own driveway before taking the vehicle out on the street. Johnson replied that that wouldn't be necessary because "there ain't a machine made I can't handle."

Johnson headed the motorcycle into the street and began to drive home. He took the most direct route although that took him through a heavily populated part of town. As he approached a red light, he became confused as to the motorcycle's controls and applied what he thought was the brake. In fact, it was the gear shift pedal.

The cycle ran through the red light and into the pedestrian crosswalk, where it struck Plaintiff Smith, who sustained a broken arm.

Smith subsequently filed suit against Johnson in county court, alleging negligence.

At trial the judge instructed the jury that if they found the defendant had not followed the standard of care of a reasonably prudent driver, he should be found liable. But if, on the other hand, he was as careful as could be expected, given his inexperience, then he should be found not liable. The jury found he was not liable.

Plaintiff objected to this instruction as an incorrect statement of the law and has based his appeal on that alleged error.

The learned trial judge's statement of the standard of care of a driver in a negligence action is correct so far as it goes. It has long been settled in this state that a defendant will be held to the standard of care of a reasonably prudent driver in avoiding harm to others; if he does not, he will be deemed negligent.

However, the judge below failed to take into account the additional fact that the defendant here injured the plaintiff during a crime—to wit, running a red light. The aforementioned rule is qualified to this effect: If a defendant breaches a statutory duty to the plaintiff, who is injured thereby, the defendant is to be held liable per se, that is, automatically, without any consideration of whether or not his conduct is reasonable.

Thus, the case must be remanded for new trial with instructions that if the jury finds the defendant was criminally culpable of running a red light and the plaintiff was injured by that act, the jury must as a matter of law find for the plaintiff.

It is so ordered.

Once again, we'll mark the various sections for the brief, as you would do on your second reading:

Smith v. *Johnson*
Supreme Court of Zed
183 Zed 2nd 14 (1983)

Procedure: Justice J. This case is before us on appeal from a verdict in the county court, entered in favor of defendant. Plaintiff appeals.

The question presented in this negligence action is a simple one: *Issue:* Does the violation of a statutory duty impose an automatic finding of negligence upon a driver?

Procedure: Plaintiff alleges error in the trial court's instructions to the jury regarding the standard of care to be followed by the defendant motorcyclist.

Decision: We agree with the plaintiff and so vacate the verdict and remand the case with instructions for a new trial.

Facts: On October 3, James Johnson bought a Honda 350 motorcycle. It was a used machine, and he purchased it for $1,000 cash from one Peter Dudley, who had himself purchased it new from a dealer outside the state. Johnson had previously driven a motorcycle only once—when he was overseas with the armed forces, stationed in Germany. That machine was a BMW. The controls of a BMW are similar to those of a Honda, but they are not identical.

After purchasing the motorcycle, Johnson started it and began to drive it home. Dudley stopped him and asked him if he (Johnson) wanted Dudley to drive it home for him. In that way Johnson could practice in his own driveway before taking the vehicle out on the street. Johnson replied that that wouldn't be necessary because "there ain't a machine made I can't handle."

Johnson headed the motorcycle into the street and began to drive home. He took the most direct route although that took him through a heavily populated

Facts: part of town. As he approached a red light, he became confused as to the motorcycle's controls and applied what he thought was the brake. In fact, it was the gear shift pedal.

The cycle ran through the red light and into the pedestrian crosswalk, where it struck Plaintiff Smith, who sustained a broken arm.

Procedure: Smith subsequently filed suit against Johnson in county court, alleging negligence.

At trial the judge instructed the jury that if they found the defendant had not followed the standard of care of a reasonably prudent driver, he should be found liable. But if, on the other hand, he was as careful as could be expected, given his inexperience, then he should be found not liable. The jury found he was not liable.

Plaintiff objected to this instruction as an incorrect statement of the law and has based his appeal on that alleged error.

Rule/Analysis: The learned trial judge's statement of the standard of care of a driver in a negligence action is correct so far as it goes. It has long been settled in this state that a defendant will be held to the standard of care of a reasonably prudent driver in avoiding harm to others; if he does not, he will be deemed negligent.

However, the judge below failed to take into account the additional fact that the defendant here injured the plaintiff during a crime—to wit, running a red light. The aforementioned rule is qualified to this effect: If a defendant breaches a statutory duty to the plaintiff, who is injured thereby, the defendant is to be held liable per se, that is, automatically, without any consideration of whether or not his conduct is reasonable.

Thus, the case must be remanded for new trial with instructions that if the jury finds the defendant was criminally culpable of running a red light and the plaintiff was injured by that act, the jury must as a matter of law find for the plaintiff.

It is so ordered.

And now the LCM brief:

SMITH V. *JOHNSON*, SUP. CT. OF ZED, 1983
FACTS:

- *D/A'ee bought cycle.*
- *While driving home, got confused, ran red light.*
- *Hit Pl/A'nt, broke his arm.*

PROCEDURE:

- *Pl/A'nt sued for negligence.*
- *Trial judge's instructions to jury: If D/A'ee didn't follow standard of care of reason. prud. person, he should be liable. If he was careful, then no liability.*
- *Verdict for D/A'ee.*
- *Pl/A'nt appealed, claiming wrong standard of liability.*

ISSUE:

- *In negligence action, what standard of care will a driver who runs red light be held to in determining if he is liable to a plaintiff injured by him?*

DECISION:

- *For Pl/A'ee; remanded for new trial.*

RULE/ANALYSIS:

The general rule as to standard of care in negligence is that driver must act as a reasonably prudent person in avoiding harm to others; if not, he's negligent.

But there is an exception: If a person breaches a statutory duty, that person will be liable automatically to anyone injured by that breach (will be liable "per se").

Here, if the D/A'ee breached a statutory duty by running a red light, he will be liable per se.

HOLDING

When a motorcycle driver is guilty of running a red light and hurts a pedestrian in the process, the driver will be liable for negligence per se because of his breach of statutory duty.

SAMPLE BRIEF FROM CRIMINAL LAW CLASS

Here is another decision from a court in the tristate area. I won't circle the various parts of the decision that correspond to sections in your brief. You try it this time.

People v. *Smith*
Supreme Court of Fred
55 S.E. 2d 258 (1988)

Jones, J. This is an appeal from a conviction of assault in the second degree. For the reasons set forth below, we hold for the defendant and order his conviction set aside.

On September 12 last year, the defendant was walking

with an acquaintance (Jones) down a street in Fredtown. Jones owed the defendant a considerable sum of money but had not been able to repay any of it for months, claiming he was virtually penniless. The defendant testified that he had given up any chance of collecting the money and had forgotten about it.

As the two men walked along the street, Doe came up to them and began harassing Jones about money he owed to Doe. Doe began shoving Jones and when Jones struck out at Doe, Doe severely beat him. Smith, a man much larger than Doe and an experienced amateur boxer, did nothing to help Jones. He did not summon the police.

After a resident of a nearby building called 911, the police arrived and gave chase to Doe, who escaped. Upon learning the facts, they did, however, arrest Smith for aiding and abetting the assault. He was charged with assault in the second degree.

At trial, the judge instructed the jury that if they found that the Defendant Smith was present at the scene of the attack and was offered a reasonable opportunity to prevent the crime, then they should find the defendant guilty of aiding and abetting an assault. The jury so found. The defendant was sentenced to five years in prison. He has appealed this conviction, which we now reverse.

The question before the court is this: Can a crime of aiding and abetting be made out merely by showing that the defendant had a reasonable opportunity to act to prevent the primary crime, in this case, an assault?

We must answer no.

It has long been settled that failure to act can indeed constitute aiding and abetting (*State* v. *Marks*, 29 S.E. 234 (1890), in which case the defendant, one of two men intent on beating their former employer, failed to open a back door to the shop in which his co-defendant was attacking the victim. The door would have allowed the victim to escape.). However, it is also settled law that such omission must be accompanied by the requisite criminal mental state, or mens rea. In the *Marks* case, it was the intent of the defendant to do harm to the victim, and this—coupled with his failure to act—constituted aiding and abetting.

In the instant case, Defendant Smith may or may not have had this criminal intent. No evidence was offered at trial as to his mental state and the jury was offered no instruction regarding it. The judge's instructions went only to the issue of failure to act. Accordingly, we set aside the conviction and order a new trial.

STATE v. *SMITH*, SUP. CT. FRED, 1988

FACTS:

- *D was present at the beating of a man.*
- *D did nothing to help, although he could have with little risk to himself.*

PROCEDURE:

- *D was arrested and charged with aiding and abetting.*
- *Judge instructed the jury that if he had an opportunity to act to prevent the assault and didn't, he was guilty of aiding and abetting.*
- *Jury convicted him.*
- *D appealed.*

ISSUE:

- *Can a person be guilty of aiding and abetting for his failure to act?*

DECISION:

- *For D. Conviction overturned, new trial ordered.*

RULE/ANALYSIS:

Although one can be found guilty of aiding and abetting by his omissions as well as by his acts, he must in such a case also have the requisite criminal intent (mens rea), i.e., the intention to cause the victim harm. Without this intent, omissions alone cannot be criminal.

Here, it is not clear whether D had the requisite intent, so the conviction must be overturned.

HOLDING:

When a man witnesses another man being beaten, his failure to stop the attack, even though it is within his power to do so, will not constitute the crime of aiding and abetting an assault if it is not proven at trial that he had criminal intent to cause the victim harm.

Recap 1   The Brief

The brief is a synopsis of a court decision you have been assigned to read for class. The purpose of briefing is to allow you to learn a rule of law and the fact situation in which it arises and to be able to recite and discuss the case if called upon by your professor in class.

The brief is composed of these elements:

1. The case name, court deciding the case, and the year of the opinion.

2. The facts—only the relevant ones, presented one per line.

3. The procedural history of the case—its journey through the maze of the court system from the time the plaintiff first filed suit until the decision was appealed.

4. The issues—the legal questions the court is being asked to resolve.

5. The decision—who the appeals court decides should win and whether the lower court should be reversed, retry the case, and so on.

6. The rule/analysis—the guiding principle the court has selected from prior law or statutes (or has made up on its own) and the application of that rule to the facts in the dispute.

7. The holding—the combination of facts and rule of law that represents the precedential value for which the case stands.

Chapter Eight

⚖ The Course Outline: Purpose and Contents

*[For a preview of this chapter,
see Recap 2 on p. 120]*

Thomas Mann says in *The Magic Mountain,* "Order and simplification are the first steps toward the mastery of a subject." The essence of the LCM approach to legal study is to bring order and simplification to your study habits, and it is through the course outline that this is done.

Case briefing, note taking, and reading and digesting outside material are only preliminary steps in the law school learning process. These activities—your daily assignments—are only half the job. From them you get only disorganized, often redundant or contradictory, raw materials. It is the process of outlining and outlining alone that converts this mass of information into a streamlined, usable form.

This chapter will tell you what the value of an outline is, what it should include, and how it should be organized. The following chapter will tell you how to actually assemble and write your outline.

THE POWER OF THE OUTLINE: ONE SOURCE FOR ALL YOUR INFORMATION

What specifically can an outline do for you?

1. An outline will aid your learning skills immeasurably. We assimilate and memorize information much better when

that material is found in a single, uniformly organized source. Your courses will require you to gather information from lectures, cases, and outside sources. Studying for an examination by trying to reread these disparate materials will be difficult and inefficient if you don't consolidate those materials into a single source.

2. An outline forces you to find the essence of a subject of law in a way case briefing and reading textbooks or notes can't. Why? Because writing outlines is hard work. You want to get the thing finished and get on with your studying. To do so, you'll have to cut out the surplus. Find the kernel, the essence of the law, discard the rest, and move on.

3. Making an outline gives you an opportunity to see what you don't know and to find out that what you thought you knew you actually don't. Your case brief seems to say the rule is X, your professor seemed to say it was Y, and the law review article you read on the matter was so confusing you were left in a complete muddle. Outlining allows you to spot these areas of garbled input in plenty of time to find out the correct answer.

4. An outline will clarify organizational problems. Professors and textbooks are not going to give you the wrong information, but they may not present it in the order that reflects the way the law actually is. By thinking about the topics, juggling them, and rearranging them in proper order, you'll have a much better understanding of how they relate.

5. Creating an outline is long-term exam studying. Without consciously trying to, your efforts at outlining will teach you the law.

YOUR OUTLINE'S CONTENTS

Your "master outline," the key document from which you will study for your exams, is a consolidation of material from three sources:

- Your case briefs
- Your class notes
- Your notes from outside reading

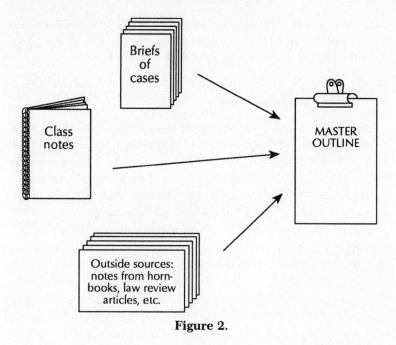

Figure 2.

The outlining process requires you to copy information from these sources into your master outline. You then set aside the notebooks containing those original materials and never refer to them again. The master outline, and that alone, will contain every bit of information you will or might be responsible for on the exam.

Your outline will contain three types of information (which do *not* correspond to the above-mentioned three sources for that information). Your outline will be made up of:

- General principles
- Rules of law and facts
- Other considerations

The "General Principles" Section

This section includes material relevant to the course, but which you won't be tested on. For instance, I always put into my General Principles section definitions of terms, the history of the area of law, what source books dealing with this subject are available, important articles on the topic, and so on. It is for your own personal knowledge.

The "Rules of Law and Facts" Section

The essence, and the bulk, of your outline will be the rules of law you have learned and short fact patterns that will help you recognize when to apply those rules. These fact patterns and rules should be written out in complete, prose sentences.[1]

(Note that you don't actually label this section of the outline "Rules of Law and Facts." I use that phrase here merely to let you know *what* goes in this section. The actual title will be the subject of law you are describing, such as "Negligence," "Commerce Clause," "Formation of Contracts," and so forth.)

Here's an example of how you would write the rule of law from a course called "Remedies," which deals with methods by which a wronged party can vindicate harm suffered:

> *II. Remedies*
> > *B. Equitable remedies*
> > > *1. General principles*
> > > > *a. Factual context*
> > > > *b. Rule*
> > > > *Equitable remedies are available to the Pl when he has no adequate legal remedies or when the existing legal remedies wouldn't make the Pl whole after the D's wrongdoing.*

In addition to the rule, I included the factual context in which the rule applies. This is very important because it helps you recognize when the rules of law should be applied.

> *B. Equitable remedies*
> > *1. General rule*
> > > *a. Factual context*
> > > *P is a collector of Van Gogh paintings; D is going to*

---

[1] However, write succinctly and use abbreviations for common legal expressions that keep recurring, such as plaintiff ("Pl"), defendant ("D"), common law ("c/l"), contract ("K"—yes, for some reason contract is abbreviated K), breach of contract ("B/K"), and so on.

The Importance of Facts

When you write your outline, always include a factual scenario with each legal rule. By doing so, you will be able to spot issues on your exams by comparing those fact patterns to the ones you have included in your outline.

Here's a rule of law that might appear in your outline on trusts and wills:

> b. Rule
> The mere fact that two persons' wills are mutual and contain reciprocal provisions does not render the wills irrevocable, but the parties can expressly agree to make the wills irrevocable.

What on earth does that mean?

Your understanding of this arcane rule will improve when you picture the factual situation in which the rule is applied. A spouse has been married before and has two children by his first marriage. He remarries and has another child by his second wife. He and this second wife make wills. They are called mutual because each spouse agrees to leave their estate to the other. The last surviving spouse agrees to leave the goodies to the three children. In other words, the husband's will says, "I leave it all to you, dear spouse, unless you die first, in which case I leave everything to the three kids." Her will says the same thing. So the effect is that the estate ultimately goes to the three children after both parents die.

Late one night the husband, after one too many tequila sunrises, races an express Amtrak and loses. His widow gets his money. But after a brief period of mourning she decides he was a creep and that the children of his first marriage are junior creeps. She wants her natural child to get all the money. So she changes her will, leaving everything to her own child.

The two children who've been cut out of the will hire a lawyer who comes up with the mutual wills rule: "Hold on, lady," he says, "those two wills were 'mutual.' Because they contained reciprocal provisions, the wills also implied a promise not to cut out the two children after the husband died."

Now, *that* is the concrete occurrence behind the mutual wills rule. It is no longer an abstract jumble of fancy words. On an exam, when a question asks about two people whose wills have similar provisions in them, one dying, and the other changing his will, then you'll know automatically this is probably a mutual wills situation.

Here's how that portion of your wills outline would read:

G. Revocability of wills
   5. Mutual wills
      a. Factual context
         H & W make wills at same time, leaving estate to other spouse then to children. After one spouse dies, the survivor tries to change his or her own will to leave estate to somebody else. Children who got cut out of survivor's will challenge, claiming the will is irrevocable.
      b. Rule
         The mere fact that two persons' wills are mutual and contain reciprocal provisions does not render them irrevocable, but the parties can expressly agree to make the wills irrevocable.

sell him one, then refuses. P sues for equit. rem. of specific performance because the painting is one of a kind. He wants the painting not $ damages.
   b. Rule
      Equitable remedies are available to the Pl when he has no adequate legal remedies or when the existing legal remedies wouldn't make the Pl whole after the D's wrongdoing.

The "Other Considerations" Section

Following the rules of law and facts section will be a section that concludes your outline. I call it "Other Considerations." Into this section goes information that you will try to add to your exam answer for extra credit (you'll see how to do this in the chapter on taking exams). Although you *could* answer the exam question correctly without any of this material, by adding it you will be demonstrating to your professor that you have gone to that extra effort worthy of meriting an A.

Examples of this extra credit might be something a professor mentioned in class—for instance, the underlying public policy behind a rule of law, a bit of legal philosophy, or a controversy in the field of law you're being tested on. In answering an exam question I often tried to slip in at least one or two sentences about how well-known legal scholars or judges would react to an issue.

Here is an example from torts class:

VII. *Other considerations*
   A. *Duty issue in negligence law*
      Traditional rule: A person owes a duty to others to prevent reasonably "foreseeable" or "predictable" harms. But there's a challenge to that rule: Some legal philosophers (e.g., Leon Green) think that it is better to use general social concerns for human welfare and the burden on the court system in determining whether or not humans owe a duty to others.

For instance, on your torts exam you have a question in which a worker is injured by a defective product and sues the manufacturer of that product. You analyze the situation, present your conclusions, and find for various reasons that the manufacturer is not liable. You state this as your conclusion in your exam booklet. Although this is sufficient to answer the question, you could then add the following paragraph:

This case illustrates what Professor Leon Green and others feel is a fault of the court system. Green's position is that in determining whether the manufacturer owes a duty to the people who use its products, the court should weigh not foreseeability of harm but social factors, such as burdens on the court system and whether institutions rather than individuals should bear the brunt of injuries from defective products. Here, although the manufacturer would probably not be found liable, there is a strong social policy argument that the D, not the injured Pl, should bear the cost of the accident.

This is the kind of material that separates the A students from the others.

To summarize, your outline will contain the following sections:

I. General principles
   Those topics you wish to include for your own understanding but that you won't be tested on.
II. Rules of law and facts in the first area covered in class
   The rules as extracted from your notes and the fact situations in which they apply.
III. Rules of law in the second area covered in class
IV. Rules of law in the third area covered in class
V. Other considerations
   Those topics that you will include, or try to include, in your exam answer for extra credit: public policy matters, legal philosophy as it relates to the subject, or your professor's own views.

ORGANIZATION OF YOUR OUTLINE

The overall organization of the outline is what we have just discussed: (1) general principles, (2) rules of law and facts, and (3) other considerations. This is straightforward. The internal organization of the rules of law and facts section, however, presents a challenge. In general, you should add the topics and subtopics roughly in the order in which they were presented in class. But when I say roughly, I mean it. The most valuable part of outlining is the process of reorganizing and consolidating the information you have learned, pulling apart the organization that professors and textbooks give you and reassembling it logically, with the rules and exceptions in their proper places.

For instance, in torts class, the professor may spend six sessions on the subject of negligence. Each session is devoted to an aspect of this type of tort: duty, breach, causation, damages, contributory negligence and comparative fault, and assumption of risk, which you might think should go into your outline as follows:

   A. Negligence
     1. Duty
     2. Breach
     3. Causation
     4. Damages
     5. Contributory negligence and comparative fault
     6. Assumption of risk

But to include the topics in your outline in that order is not helpful because it doesn't reflect the actual relationship among them. Those topics should be outlined in a way that illustrates how each one relates to the other:

   A. Negligence
     1. Elements of a cause of action
       a. Duty
       b. Breach
       c. Causation
       d. Damages
     2. Defenses to negligence
       a. Contributory negligence
       b. Comparative fault
       c. Assumption of risk

In addition, you may have general principles and other considerations sections that relate specifically to a subtopic such as negligence. Accordingly, your outline would include such sections too:

Torts Master Outline

   I. General principles
  II. Intentional torts
 III. Negligence
    A. General principles of negligence law
     1. History
     2. Relation to intentional torts
     3. Statutes overriding common law
     4. Sources of law
     5. Bar associations groups representing negligence lawyers

    B. *Elements of a cause of action in negligence*
       1. *Duty*
       2. *Breach*
       3. *Causation*
       4. *Damages*
    C. *Defenses to negligence*
       1. *Contributory negligence*
       2. *Comparative fault*
       3. *Assumption of risk*
    D. *Other considerations in negligence law*
       1. *The controversy over comparative fault*
       2. *The use of expert witnesses in negl. cases*
VIII. *Other considerations in tort law in general*
    A. *Foreseeability as an issue in tort law*
    B. *Legislative reforms in the insurance industry*

We will turn now to several examples of organizing the many topics you'll have in a law school course and putting them into an order that is most helpful to you.

ORGANIZATION—EXAMPLE ONE

Let's take remedies as an example. Remember, these are techniques that the law has devised for vindicating wrongs. Major remedies are the following:

- damages
- specific performance
- ejectment
- constructive trust
- replevin

But to simply add these remedies to your outline in this order is not helpful. The more efficient way is to categorize them in the way that reflects the actual state of the law:

    A. *Legal remedies*
       1. *Damages*

    2. *Replevin*
    3. *Ejectment*
  B. *Equitable remedies*
    1. *Specific performance*
    2. *Constructive trust*

Adding your general principles section would give you this organization:

  A. *Legal remedies*
    1. *General principles of legal remedies*
    2. *The major legal remedies*
      a. *Damages*
      b. *Replevin*
      c. *Ejectment*
  B. *Equitable remedies*
    1. *General principles of equitable remedies*
    2. *The major equitable remedies*
      a. *Specific performance*
      b. *Constructive trust*

ORGANIZATION—EXAMPLE TWO

During your first-year torts class, you'll learn about intentional torts—wrongs committed by someone who acted with the purpose of causing harmful consequences. There are various types of these torts: assault, battery, false imprisonment, and a few others, each of which is made up of different elements that a plaintiff has to prove in order to win a case. In addition, you'll learn a number of defenses that excuse the bad behavior of one accused of such a tort.

You could organize this portion of your torts outline as follows, simply listing the definitions and defenses for each tort:

 II. *Intentional torts*
  A. *General principles*
  B. *Specific intentional torts*
    1. *Assault*
      a. *Defined*
      b. *Defenses*

> 2. *Battery*
>   a. *Defined*
>   b. *Defenses*

And so on, for each one.

It would be much better, however, to organize in such a way that you consolidate as much material as possible. You could do that here, because—as you'll soon learn in class—the defenses to all of the intentional torts are virtually the same.

> II. *Intentional torts*
>   A. *General principles*
>   B. *Elements of a plaintiff's cause of action*
>   1. *Assault*
>   2. *Battery*
>   3. *False imprisonment*
>   C. *Defenses to be raised by the defendant*
>   1. *Consent*
>   2. *Self-defense*
>   3. *Justification*

ORGANIZATION—EXAMPLE THREE

The course is real property; the subject under discussion is landlord-tenant law. The rules you have learned as to a landlord's right against a defaulting tenant are these (presented, incidentally, in the same order in which they were taught in an actual real property class):

> 1. *The common-law rule of damages a landlord may recover*
> 2. *Availability and mechanics of liquidated damages*
> 3. *Use of acceleration clauses*
> 4. *Legal means by which to continue a tenant's liability after default*
> 5. *Methods to oust a defaulting tenant (self-help, ejectment, summary proceedings)*
> 6. *Use of default clauses in summary proceedings*

7. *Drafting default clauses from a landlord's point of view*
8. *Majority rule on landlord's rights when tenant abandons the premises*
9. *Minority rule on tenant's abandonment*
10. *Majority rule on landlord's right to relet abandoned property*
11. *Minority rule on reletting*
12. *Commercial frustration excusing tenant's obligations*
13. *Eminent domain excusing tenant's obligations*
14. *Public policy considerations*

Of course, these rules mean little to you now. But in glancing at them you can see certain parallel topics and some broad categories that might embrace several of the rules. Finding such categories and parallels is what outlining is all about. Here's the way to organize this material:

V. *Default by tenant: Landlord's rights*
   A. *Recoverable damages in suit by landlord*
      1. *Common-law rule*
      2. *Modern rule*
         a. *Liquidated damages*
         b. *Survival of tenant's liability for rent*
         c. *Acceleration clauses*
   B. *Ousting a defaulting tenant*
      1. *Self-help*
      2. *Ejectment*
      3. *Summary proceedings*
         a. *Use of default clauses to permit summary proceedings*
         b. *How to draft clauses*
   C. *Remedies of landlord on tenant's abandonment*
      1. *General rule on landlord's remedies*
         a. *Majority*
         b. *Minority*
      2. *Landlord's right to relet property*
         a. *Majority*
         b. *Minority*

    D. *Excuse of tenant's obligations*
      1. *Commercial frustration*
      2. *Eminent domain*
    E. *Other considerations*
      Public policy issues in landlord-tenant relations

THE FINER POINTS OF OUTLINING

Case Names

Should you include case names in your outline? (And, by implication, should you memorize them for the test?) In some courses, case names are synonymous with major doctrines and rules of law. Learning them and using them on the exam will be a good shorthand way to let your professor know you recognize a parallel situation. You can save much space and time in writing your exam answer by using such case names.

In other courses, case names are less valuable. In contracts, for instance, there are a few landmark decisions standing for propositions so clearly that they are synonymous with the rule applied in them. Most cases in contracts, torts, and real property are merely illustrations of the rule. So, just because the case you read for class on the subject of manifestation of an offer was *In re Dolt's Zucchini,* this does not mean that lawyers throughout the country uniformly refer to the proposition as the *Dolt's Zucchini* rule.

In your outline, then, put only those case names that are widely identified with the legal rule. The case name might make up the topic heading:
    4. *The* Erie *Doctrine*
Or you might indicate the case name parenthetically since very few legal rules actually take their names from a landmark decision.
    4. *Federal courts' application of state laws (the* Erie *Doctrine)*

Statutes

The law in this country is only partly (and to a lesser and lesser degree every year) found solely in court cases. Many statutes now govern where only the common law (the court-determined law) once ruled. In all of your courses, you will be responsible for rules of law found in statutes.

These statutes represent the most arcane and convoluted legal writing you will ever encounter. Still, it is to your advantage to digest statutory passages that have been assigned or that are relevant to your course and to include them in your outline.

For example, here's a section from an actual statute—the Illinois Civil Practice Act (CPA):

38. Counterclaims. (1) Subject to rules, any demand by one or more defendants against one or more plaintiffs, or against one or more co-defendants, whether in the nature of setoff, recoupment, crossbill in equity, cross demand or otherwise, and whether in tort or contract, for liquidated or unliquidated damages, or for other relief, may be pleaded as a cross demand in any action and when so pleaded shall be called a counterclaim.

This mouthful would look something like this in your outline:

IV. Pleadings
    C. Counterclaims
        1. Statutory rule—Section 38, CPA
           Any claim of any nature by any defendant against any other party in the action may be pleaded as a cross demand. It's called a counterclaim.

Length

How long should your outline be? The answer is: long enough to include every bit of information that you might be tested on in your exam. Not a word more or a word less. Be sure to ask your professor exactly what's fair game for the exam.

Your outline should include:

- All the rules of law the professor might test you on
- Factual scenarios corresponding to each of those rules

- Important case names and their holdings
- Digests of relevant statutory provisions
- The "general principles" and "other considerations" material you consider important

My outlines averaged about 35 to 40 pages of handwritten, legal-size paper. To keep it to this size, you must be very concise—boil all the rules of law, factual scenarios, and other considerations down to their essence. A ten-page case that has been turned by you into a two-page brief must be further distilled into a 30-word rule of law.

For a summary of the outlining process described in this chapter, please see Recap 2 on page 120.

Chapter Nine

⚖ The Course Outline: Putting It All Together

[For a preview of this chapter, see Recap 2 on p. 120]

STEP ONE: THE SOURCE OUTLINE

About three or four weeks after classes start, you should begin the outlining process. It is essential to start early. If you wait until the week prior to an exam, you won't have enough time to create a useful outline.

The first step is to write a one- or two-page "source outline." This document is an outline of the topic and subtopic headings that will appear in your master outline. Under each heading you'll jot down where you can find the rule of law about that topic (the name of the case that dealt with that topic, the pages in your class notebook, the date of the lecture your professor discussed it, and the pages of any outside reading you did on the topic). The source outline does *not* include any rules of law; it simply contains brief notations as to *where* in your sources you can find those rules and any other information you want to include.

The source outline serves two purposes. First, it helps you organize the topics and subtopics before you start writing. Second, it serves as a guide to writing your master outline.

To make this source outline, you need several pieces of legal-size paper, a pencil or erasable pen, and a list of the major topics covered in class to date. A syllabus is the most handy, but you might also use the table of contents of your

111

casebook or even a commercial outline. Using this list, write the major headings, leaving plenty of space between each. Under these write the various subheads.

An example of your contracts source outline would look like this:

II. Offer and acceptance
   A. Offer
     1. Defined

     2. Distinguished from invitations to offer

Once you have added all the topics in an order you feel comfortable with, assemble your sources. If your notebooks are not paginated, number the pages at this point. Then, under each topic, write a short citation to the page in each source where that topic is discussed.

Let's say the subject you're about to outline is this: How an offer to enter a contract differs from an invitation to make an offer. You find discussions of this topic in the following places: pages 13 and 14 of your class notes (for this, you might use the notation "N13–14"); pages 78 and 79 in a textbook on contracts ("T78–79"); the briefs you did of the *Jones* v. *White* and the *Smith* v. *Black* cases ("*Jones*" and "*Smith*"); and pages 4 and 5 in a commercial outline ("O4–5"). Put these notations under the topic headings in your source outline:

  A. Offer
    2. Distinguished from invitations to offer N13, Jones, Smith, *T78–79, O4–5*

STEP TWO: THE MASTER OUTLINE

Once you have noted in your source outline where all the information you wish to incorporate into your master outline is located, the hard work is over.

Now, you simply read the material in your three sources, consolidate it into a single factual context and a single rule of law, and write that down in your master outline.

Let's walk through an example of the process.

In contract law there is a concept called "consideration." In U.S. and English law, a contract can be enforced only if there is consideration, meaning each party to a contract must do something he isn't otherwise obligated to—pay some money, engage in an act, make a promise to act or refrain from acting, give the other party an object. The law says that this consideration can be very insignificant, but it must be present for the contract to be enforceable.

In contracts class your professor finishes with the subject of consideration and moves on to other topics. You want to include this subject in your master outline. The following is an example of how the outline might look:

This is your source outline:

II. Formation of contracts
  B. Consideration
    N23, T435, Haigh *v.* Brooks

In writing your master outline, you turn to N23 (page 23 of your class notes) and find the following:

Millionaire recluse—tired of oil wells he owns—says to X, "Give me one dollar—you take wells." X says okay. Millionaire's wife hears of this and says no way. Millionaire backs out and X sues. Court says: X gets oil wells. Amount of consideration not important.

Now you turn to page 435 of the textbook *Contracts Made Simple*. There is this passage:

The general rule both in this country and in England is that any detriment to the promisee, no matter how small it may seem from an economic standpoint, is sufficient to support a promise and qualify as consideration to render a contract enforceable. Absent fraud, courts will not inquire into the fairness of a contract.

Finally, you turn to your case briefs and look up *Haigh* v. *Brooks*. Your holding is as follows:

When the D promises to pay Pl a sum of money if Pl hands over what the D thinks is a valid note obligating D but in fact is invalid, a contract is formed and the D must pay the sum he had promised. A court will not look at the value of the consideration and even the physical act of handing to the D a worthless piece of paper is sufficient consideration.

Although they say so in different ways, each of these sources presents the same concept. This, then, is what you would write in your master outline:

> II. *Formation of contracts*
> > B. *Consideration*
> > > 1. *Factual context: Two people make a contract but the performances under that contract are very unequal. One must do or pay much more than the other. Is this an enforceable contract?*
> > > 2. *Rule*
> > > *The amount or degree of consideration is irrelevant. Unless there is fraud, a promise will be enforceable as long as the promisee agrees to do or give up anything at all.*

Subtopics

You'll find that in order to include all the requisite information, your outline will often contain very small categories and subtopics. This is especially true in classes such as contracts and constitutional law, in which there is a great deal of law to learn. For these sub-subtopics, you'll probably wish to give up on formal outline procedure and just use bullets or dashes to mark the points:

> C. *Termination and revocation of offer*
> > 3. *Revocation*
> > > a. *Revocation by communication*
> > > *"The rule is . . ."*
> > > b. *Revocation of offers for rewards*
> > > *"The rule is . . ."*
> > > c. *Revocation of divisible offers*
> > > *"The rule is . . ."*
> > > d. *Irrevocable offers*
> > > > (1) *Option defined*
> > > > *"An option is . . ."*

(2) *Majority rule*
  "The rule is . . ."
(3) *Uniform Commercial Code*
  • *Applies only with sales of goods*
  • *Applies everywhere but Louisiana*
  • *Rule*
    "The rule is . . ."

SOME NUTS AND BOLTS OF OUTLINING

Paper

Write your outline on legal-size lined paper. The longer size is preferable because it reduces ultimate page length. Don't use a spiral notebook; you'll have to insert material from time to time. To keep the pages together, use rubber bands or a large clamp.

Table of Contents

It may be helpful to write a one- or two-page table of contents for your outline. This not only gives you a helpful guide as to what your outline contains, but—if you fill it in every time you write a portion of the outline—it is valuable as an indicator of what you have outlined so far and what remains to be done.

Don't Miss Anything

Once you have transferred the information from your notebooks and case briefs into the master outline, place a checkmark next to or draw a line through that material where it appears in the notebooks and briefs. The purpose of doing this is so that you will be able to thumb through the original sources quickly and see if there is anything you have neglected to put in your outline.

Safety First

For security's sake, always make a copy of the outline when you have finished a section. Keep this copy in a location separate from the original. The amount of time and effort you put into your outline (and the fact that it will be the sole document used for exam studying) makes keeping an extra copy very important.

Cross Referencing

If you are ambitious you may wish for completeness's sake to key the rule in your outline to the source material in your notebooks and briefs. This involves making simple notations in the margins of the outline next to each rule, indicating from which source you have extracted the information that appears in your master outline. For instance, you would write merely "N4, T29, *Jones*" just as you did for your source outline, to indicate that the information appearing in that spot in the outline came from page 4 of your notes, page 29 of a textbook on the subject, and your brief of the *Jones* v. *Black* case.

The purpose of doing this is to verify the accuracy of the material if you run into a conflict later with, say, a fellow student's conception of the rule.

How Often?

You should update your master outline every three weeks or so. If you wait much longer than a month, the task becomes overly burdensome. I would also recommend that you stagger your outlining efforts so that you don't have to outline four or five courses on the same weekend.

Legal Schematics

When you have completed a section of the outline, you might want to schematize the area of law with which that portion of the outline deals. A legal schematic is nothing more than a line diagram indicating the movement of legal activity, usually chronologically, or showing the relationship of one legal rule to another.

These diagrams are extremely helpful in assisting you to understand particularly complicated areas of the law.

The diagram on page 118 is part of the schematic I did for my civil procedure class. It deals with the pretrial portion of the class. The rules referred to are the federal rules of civil procedure.

These, then, are the mechanics of creating a master outline. To give you an idea of what one actually looks like, here is a portion of one of my outlines—from Torts II:

V. *Products liability*

A. *General principles*

1. *History of products liability*

Winterbottom, N34

a. Winterbottom *v.* Wright *(1842)*

Seller of a product owed duty only to those with whom seller was in contractual relation (called privity), that is, only owed duty to immediate purchaser. And only duty if seller did something wrong—was negligent.

N37–38, T285

b. *1890s*

Social movement to improve food and drug industries. Courts said manufacturers should stand behind their food and drug products. But courts weren't sure how to impose a legal duty, so they borrowed from contract law and said that manufacturers gave an implied warranty that the products were fit.

MacPherson, N39

c. MacPherson *v.* Buick *(1916)*

Cordozo expanded negligence rule, holding that if it were reasonably foreseeable that the product would harm someone if defective, the manufacturer would be liable for the harm.

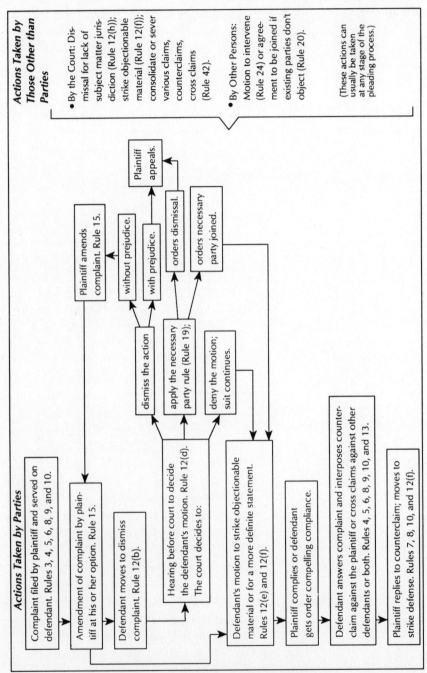

Actions Taken by Those Other than Parties

- By the Court: Dismissal for lack of subject matter jurisdiction (Rule 12(h)); strike objectionable material (Rule 12(f)); consolidate or sever various claims, counterclaims, cross claims (Rule 42).

- By Other Persons: Motion to intervene (Rule 24) or agreement to be joined if existing parties don't object (Rule 20).

  (These actions can usually be taken at any stage of the pleading process.)

Actions Taken by Parties

Complaint filed by plaintiff and served on defendant. Rules 3, 4, 5, 6, 8, 9, and 10.

Amendment of complaint by plaintiff at his or her option. Rule 15.

Defendant moves to dismiss complaint. Rule 12(b).

Hearing before court to decide the defendant's motion. Rule 12(d). The court decides to:

Defendant's motion to strike objectionable material or for a more definite statement. Rules 12(e) and 12(f).

Plaintiff complies or defendant gets order compelling compliance.

Defendant answers complaint and interposes counterclaim against the plaintiff or cross claims against other defendants or both. Rules 4, 5, 6, 8, 9, 10, and 13.

Plaintiff replies to counterclaim; moves to strike defense. Rules 7, 8, 10, and 12(f).

Plaintiff amends complaint. Rule 15.

without prejudice.

with prejudice.

Plaintiff appeals.

orders dismissal.

orders necessary party joined.

dismiss the action

apply the necessary party rule (Rule 19);

deny the motion; suit continues.

Figure 3.   Schematic—Civil Procedure

Henningsen, *N39, T287*	d. Henningsen *v.* Bloomfield Motors *(1960)*
	Court extended implied warranty to all goods and to all persons injured whether or not there was privity of contract
Greenman, *N39*	e. Greenman *v.* Yuba Power Products *(1963)*
	Justice Traynor developed a new theory—strict products liability. He discarded warranty concept.
Restat. 402A	f. *Restatement of Torts (2d) Section 402A (1965)*
	Adopted a version of strict products liability similar to Traynor's in the Greenman *case. After that, nearly all states used the Restatement as a model for a theory of strict products liability. Warranty is still used, but not necessary.*
Greenman, *N39, T290*	D. *Strict product liability*
	1. *Factual context: A product (stove, car, drug, tool, etc.) has hurt a consumer or a bystander. The issue is whether the injured party can sue the manufacturer or the other sellers (such as the wholesaler and retailer) for the harm.*
	2. *Rules of liability*
Greenman, *N39, T291*	a. *Traynor's rule: A manufacturer is strictly liable in tort when it puts a product on the market knowing it will be used without inspection for defects, proves to have a defect that causes an injury to the buyer or bystander.*

Restat. 402A

b. *Restatement of Torts (2d) Section 402A*

   (1) *Rule: One who sells a defective product unreasonably dangerous to the user or consumer or property is liable for physical harm if (a) the seller is engaged in the business of selling, and (b) the product is expected to and does reach the consumer in the condition in which it is sold.*

   (2) *Rule applies even though seller is not negligent and there is no privity between the manufacturer and the injured party.*

N39–40

   (3) *This is majority rule.*

N39–41, 067, T295

   (4) *Limitation: Not as "strict" as name suggests. Some courts have backed away from imposing too much liability on manufacturers by finding products that cause harm are not necessarily "defective."*

c. *Statutory developments*

N42–43

   (1) *Uniform Products Liability Act. This is a uniform state law . . .*

Recap 2   The Course Outline

1. The course outline is a concise synthesis of all the rules of law for which you will be responsible on the examination, as well as supplemental information you feel you should be aware of (some of which you might include in your exam answer, and some is simply to increase your understanding of the topic).

2. The sources that you will use to write your outline include the following, contained in your spiral-bound notebooks:

- Class notes
- Briefs of cases
- Textbooks (hornbooks) and commercially prepared outlines and briefs, law review articles, non-case material from casebooks, major treatises, and nonlegal materials

3. The outline is to be organized as follows:

Table of Contents

I. General principles (sources of the law, bibliographies, history of the legal concepts, etc.—material you feel is important, but that you will not need to know for the exam)
II. Rules of Law and Facts—First Topic
III. Rules of Law and Facts—Second Topic
IV. Rules of Law and Facts—Third Topic
   Etc.
V. Other considerations (public policy considerations, professor's views on a subject, academic or philosophical controversies relating to the area of law you have been studying—material that you will try to include on the exam for extra credit once you have answered the question asked by the professor)

4. Assembly of your outline:

a. Find some source that contains all topic headings in the area of law you have studied for the course (a casebook or hornbook table of contents, for instance). From this and your own thoughts, write a source outline that contains topics and subtopics down to the lowercase letters. Leave plenty of space after each heading.

b. Paginate all your spiral notebooks. Go through each one separately, and mark in the space you have left under each heading on your source outline the page number of that source on which a discussion of the subject is found. Use very short notations; for instance, use "N3" to indicate that page 3 of your notes contains a discussion of the relevant subject. Go through the rest of your source notebooks and do the same.

c. Using this source outline as a guide, go back to the beginning, and begin writing your outline on loose, legal-size sheets. Refer to each topic, look up the pages noted on the source outline, synthesize a rule, and write that in your outline. Include a short statement about what fact situations the issue normally arises in. Write a narrative text but use standard abbreviations.

d. When you have formulated the rule and written it in your outline, mark through the portions of your original source materials to allow you to verify later that you haven't left out anything and to avoid duplication.

e. When finished with the material you have covered to date, add the topics to your table of contents and put the outline aside. Don't study it at this point.

f. You might want to do a legal schematic that shows the relationships between rules or the chronological progression of the legal activity under study.

5. You should begin outlining no later than one month into the semester and should outline thereafter whenever your professor comes to the end of a major topic—in any event, however, not less frequently than every four weeks. Outlining is a long process, and, if you wait too long, the project will become too unwieldy.

Chapter Ten

♎ Preparing for Exams

[For a preview of this chapter,
see Recap 3 on p. 170]

STEP ONE: READ THE MASTER OUTLINE

The bulk of the study process under the LCM system is simply stated:

Read your master outline.[1]

Read it. Don't skim it, don't memorize it. Read it. Then reread it. Don't bother to underline (if you've followed the LCM system in creating the master outline, everything you've written is important). Read the outline, visualizing the facts and understanding each rule, until you're sick of it.

Then read it again.

And again and again.

For longer courses, it may take eight hours or more to plow through the material the first time. Subsequent readings will be faster; eventually you'll find that you need only glance at a topic heading or subhead to know exactly what the fact scenario and the rule of law are without looking at your textual discussion of the rule.

Time Management

You should allow yourself at least three days of studying per course. It's best if these days are contiguous but this is often

---

[1] Everything except the general principles section, of course, which you'll recall is simply background.

not realistic, especially if you have several exams within a short time period.

If you find that you have two exams on the same day or on consecutive days, don't study for them at the same time. Do your complete studying for one test, then put that outline aside and study for the other exam until you've learned the material. (I generally preferred to study for the second exam first, and a number of other students told me that this was their game plan also.)

Here's an example: Thursday at 4 P.M. is zero hour for your contracts exam; Friday at 10 A.M. is your date with torts. You should spend Saturday, Sunday, and Monday studying torts, and Tuesday, Wednesday, and Thursday studying contracts. Thursday night (after a rest) look over the torts outline several more times.

These days of study must be free from interruptions from the outside world. No distractions. Disconnect your phone. Put a "Quarantined" sign on your door. Buy earplugs.

Don't Panic

If, for personal reasons or the logistics of your exam schedule, you cannot fit in three uninterrupted days, don't panic. I found myself in a troubling spot one time. As a transfer student I had to take courses out of normal order. This threw off my exam schedule, and I found I had three exams scheduled in the space of two days. I started the week by reading all my master outlines, but then put aside the third and turned my attention to the first two. "Just a few more hours on this one," I kept telling myself, and put off studying for the last test. The time simply got away from me, and I walked into the last of the three exams a nervous wreck, having studied a total of maybe four hours for the test.

Since I'd done a complete outline and had spent those four hours reading it in complete quiet and with as much concentration as I could muster, however, I found that I could answer the questions without any difficulty.

One word of reassurance: All law school administrators understand the pressure on first-year students around exam time. They generally schedule examinations at the expense of upper-class students to make certain that there are large blocks of time between the first-year exams to give students adequate time to prepare. Remember too that your school will also halt regular classwork about a week before the exams to allow you extra study time.

STEP TWO: CREATE THE EXAM OUTLINE

Reading your master outline, then, is essentially the study process. By doing this, you will pass the examination. But to ace a law school exam, you need to recognize *all* the issues a professor pours into the questions: Who's going to sue whom? For what? What are the defenses?

To identify these issues and to be able to write about them in a lawyerly way you must create another outline, the "exam outline." This outline is very short—just a single sheet of paper. It contains most of the major topics (excluding the general principles sections) in your master outline, arranged according to the most logical order of presentation on the exam.

When I say that it contains "topics," I mean just that: only the one-word topic heading from your outline. Not the rule, not the facts. Just the heading.

Here is an example of an actual exam outline.

Torts—Exam Outline

INTENTIONAL TORTS

   A. *Intent*
   B. *Causes of action*
     1. *Battery*
     2. *Assault*
     3. *False imprisonment*
     4. *Intentional infliction of emotional distress*
     5. *Trespass*
   C. *Defenses*
     1. *Defense of self & others*

2. *Justification*
3. *Consent*
4. *Necessity*
5. *Privilege*
6. *Mistake*

NEGLIGENCE

A. *Cause of action*
  1. *Duty*
  2. *Breach*
  3. *Causation*
  4. *Damages*
B. *Defenses*
  1. *Contributory negligence*
  2. *Comparative fault*
  3. *Assumption of risk*

DEFAMATION

A. *Cause of action*
  1. *Defamatory statement*
  2. *Inducement and innuendo*
  3. *Colloquium*
  4. *Publication*
  5. *Damages (if required)*
  6. *Fault (constitutional privilege)*
B. *Defenses*
  1. *State law privileges*
  2. *Truth*

STRICT PRODUCTS LIABILITY

A. *Cause of action*
  1. *Duty*
  2. *Cause*
  3. *Damages*
B. *Defenses*
  1. *Comparative fault*
  2. *Assumption of risk*
  3. *Misuse*

OTHER CONSIDERATIONS

    A. *Duty issue in negligence law*

    B. *Public policy behind strict products liability*

    C. *Professor Jones' views of constitutional privileges in defamation actions*

    D. *Economic analysis of tort law in general*

Why do you need an exam outline?

Because of the nature of law school exams. An exam outline provides a mental checklist that you will use as you answer your essay question to help you spot the issues. An illustration will demonstrate how important this issue-detecting game is. Let's say on your torts exam you're given the following fact pattern:

Question One

Joe, a surgeon, is walking down the street. He meets Sam on the sidewalk. Sam says to Joe: "Why, you're a lousy doctor. I'm going to kill you! I go into the hospital to have a splinter removed; next thing I know I'm on the table and you're taking out my appendix. What's more, you left a sponge in me! I can still feel it. I'm so ashamed I can't eat or sleep." He points to his stomach. A passerby says, "Yeah, you look pretty lumpy." Sam backs Joe into an alleyway from which he can't escape. Fearing for his life, Joe draws back to swing at Sam. Just then a car speeds around the corner. It's an Inflamo Deluxe driven by Myra, who is drunk and exceeding the speed limit. The car jumps the curb right in front of Sam and Joe. They leap out of the way. Myra brakes and the car strikes the building going only two miles per hour. It explodes in a ball of flames. Myra is blown free and lands on Sam, rupturing his spleen and running her stockings. Joe performs an emergency spleen repair on Sam. While he is open, Joe also removes Sam's gall bladder, not because there was anything wrong with it but because he needs the practice. Although the spleen repair is successful and he removes the sponge, Joe accidentally leaves one of Myra's stockings inside Sam when he sews him up.

Identify all the potential lawsuits that might arise out of these facts, tell who would win, and explain why.

By mentally scanning the exam outline over and over again as you read through the facts you'll be able to spot the legal issues that arise and make sure you haven't forgotten any of them. You'll see how important it is to have this outline in your head when you take a look at how many potential issues there are:

1. *Joe v. Sam*
   —*slander for calling him a lousy doctor*
   —*false imprisonment for backing him into an alleyway*
   —*intentional infliction of emotional distress for the death threat*

2. *Sam v. Joe*
   —*medical malpractice for leaving the sponge in him*
   —*assault for drawing back his fist to hit him*
   —*medical malpractice for leaving the stocking in him*
   —*medical battery for removing the gall bladder without permission*
   —*negligent infliction of emotional distress for his appearance because of the sponge*
   —*intentional infliction of emotional distress for the assault*

3. *Joe v. Myra*
   —*negligent infliction of emotional distress for the fright caused by the accident*

4. *Sam v. Myra*
   —*negligence for injury caused by auto accident*
   —*negligent infliction of emotional distress for the fright caused by the accident*

5. *Myra v. Joe*
   —*conversion of personal property for losing her stocking in Sam*

6. *Myra v. Inflamo Car Company*
   —*negligence suit for defective car:*
   —*personal injury*
   —*property damage (stockings run)*
   —*emotional distress*

—*strict products liability for defective car:*
  —*personal injury*
  —*property damage (stockings run)*
  —*emotional distress*
7. *Joe v. Inflamo Car Company*
  —*negligence suit for defective car:*
    —*personal injury*
    —*emotional distress*
  —*strict products liability for defective car:*
    —*personal injury*
    —*emotional distress*
8. *Sam v. Inflamo Car Company*
  —*negligence suit for defective car:*
    —*personal injury*
    —*emotional distress*
  —*strict products liability for defective car:*
    —*personal injury*
    —*emotional distress*

Even if you can write no more than one or two sentences about each cause of action, your professor will be extremely impressed that you were able to recognize all the issues.

Here is a second example of an exam outline:

Constitutional Law—Exam Outline

  I. *Supreme Court's authority*
    A. *Judicial review*
    B. *Review of state court decisions*
    C. *Congressional power to curtail jurisdiction*
  II. *Powers of Congress*
    A. *Implied powers and the Necessary and Proper clause*
    B. *Commerce power*
    C. *Taxing power*
    D. *Spending power*
    E. *War, treaty, foreign affairs powers*
  III. *State regulation*
    A. *Dormant Commerce Clause*
    B. *Preemption and consent by Congress*

IV. *Interstate immunities and obligations, collabor.*
   A. *Immunities*
   B. *Obligations and collaborations*
V. *Separation of powers*
   A. *National policy*
   B. *Authority of three branches*
VI. *Procedural due process*
   A. *Double jeopardy*
   B. *Self-incrimination*
   C. *Search and seizure*
   D. *Right to a jury trial*
   E. *Right to counsel*
   F. *Others*
VII. *Substantive due process*
   A. *Economic*
   B. *Noneconomic*
   C. *Eminent domain*
   D. *Contract clause*
VIII. *Civil rights*
   A. *Constitutional protections*
   B. *Statutory protections*
   C. *Congress's modification of constitut. rights*
IX. *Equal protection*
   A. *Suspect classifications*
   B. *Fundamental rights*
   C. *Irrebuttable presumptions*
X. *Freedom of expression*
   A. *Political speech*
   B. *Expression in public places*
   C. *Commercial obscenity*
   D. *Expression on private property*
   E. *Group libel*
   F. *Interference with judicial process*
   G. *Prior restraints*
   H. *Loyalty oaths and legislative inquisitions*
XI. *Freedom of religion*
   A. *Establishment clause*
   B. *Free-exercise clause*
XII. *Constitutional adjudication*

STEP THREE: MEMORIZE THE EXAM OUTLINE

What? Memorize the entire exam outline?

It won't be nearly as hard as you think. For one thing, because you've read your master outline many times you'll have practically memorized the topics already. Besides, if an actor can learn four hours of Shakespeare, a few exam outlines should be a piece of cake. It's important that these outlines be committed to memory because by mentally, even subconsciously, scanning them as you read your exam question the legal issues hidden in the question will come popping out.[2]

If memorization daunts you, try mnemonics. When you write your exam outline, try to rearrange the list of topics (to the extent you can without interfering with any necessary order) and find synonyms for words so that the first letters of the topic make a recognizable unit.

For instance, for the constitutional law outline above, I did a little rearrangement of the order of topics in the freedom of expression section and came up with the acronym: POLICE PR. This is a lucky one because one of the words (police) relates to the topic; it is often the police who enforce laws governing freedom of expression. Here is how I came up with the phrase:

Political speech
Oaths (loyalty) and legislative investigation
Libel (group)
Interference with the judicial process
Commercial obscenity
Expression in public places

Private property (expression on)
Restraints (prior)

---

[2] In memorizing your exam outline, do your best but don't worry if some of it slips away from you. The purpose of this memorization process is to help you spot issues, not recite outline topics perfectly.

STEP FOUR: LEARN THE ANSWER FORMAT

It is important to know the structure of your exam answer *before* you go into the test room. Once inside, you won't have time to waste wondering how to organize your answer.

I recommend memorizing a very short format that is so generic you can use it for any law school exam that gives you a fact pattern and asks for your legal analysis of the situation presented by those facts. These, called "problem" or "fact pattern" exams, are far and away the most common type of law school exam (for a discussion of other types of law school exams, please see the next chapter).

I offer this format below. Note that the bracketed phrases—such as [short answer]—are merely to remind you *what* to write there; they themselves are not actual headings. The nonbracketed words you should actually write in your blue book as topic headings.

> I. *[Short answer]*
> II. *Issues presented*
> III. *Analysis*
> > *Issue 1*
> > > *[Rule of law]*
> > > *[Applicable facts]*
> > > *[Conclusion]*
> > *Issue 2*
> > > *[Rule of law]*
> > > *[Applicable facts]*
> > > *[Conclusion]*
> > *[Remaining issues the same way]*
> IV. *Other considerations*
> V. *Conclusion*

What you should write under each section will be discussed in the following chapter. Your only task here is to memorize this format. You may prefer a different one, or a variation on what I suggest. What is important to remember is this: before you go into the exam, you must have a firm idea of the structure your answer will take.

OPEN-BOOK EXAMS—BEWARE
OF FALSE CONFIDENCE

There are two problems with open-book exams—one is psychological and the other is practical.

Psychologically, an open-book exam can instill a false sense of confidence that eats away at your preexam study discipline. The attitude is this: "I can coast now because I can look up the answer." But you won't be able to. Believe me. All the books, notebooks, briefs, and other papers you carry into class with you will be useless 99 percent of the time. They might even be worse than useless because you may waste so much time looking up unknown answers that you won't have time to respond to those that you *do* know, resulting in a lower grade than you deserve.

From a practical standpoint, too, open-book exams are worse because you'll be getting a much harder test, with issues more subtle and more numerous than a closed-book exam addresses.

How, then, does your study technique for one of these exams differ from that for a closed-book test?

It doesn't.

You follow exactly the same approach: write the master outline, read it over and over, write the exam outline and learn it, and memorize the answer format.

The only variation is this: paginate your master outline and make an index that includes all the topics and the pages on which the discussion of them can be found. Also, you should type or print a copy of the exam outline and the answer format and put those in the front of your master outline.

In courses where you have a large volume of statutory material (for instance, securities regulation, taxation, or corporate law), and where you anticipate the professor will question you on material in those statute books, mark all the relevant portions with yellow tabs or paperclips.

When you take an open-book exam, you should have on your table:

1. The master outline
2. An index to the master outline

3. The exam outline
4. The answer format
5. Any statutory material, as described above

Everything else should go onto the floor. But don't leave anything home. Bring it all: case briefs, notebooks, textbooks, casebooks, class notes. It has been known to happen that a student miraculously sees that the fact pattern on the exam is identical to the case described in a footnote in the casebook. It doesn't happen very often. But lugging 30 pounds of books with you is a small price to pay for a potential A.

STUDYING FROM OLD EXAMS—THE INSIDE EDGE

Nearly all law schools have exams available from prior years. They are usually found in the school library and can be checked out for a day or two or photocopied. Some professors will even hand out old copies of their exams.

An old test can be quite valuable (provided it was written by *your* professor). There are several ways to use old exams:

1. They give you general practice in taking a law school exam. After you've studied your material, sit down and see how many issues you can spot. I wouldn't actually take the whole exam (there are more efficient ways to use your study energy), but the more familiar you are with such exams, the more comfortable you will be going into yours.

2. Use them with your study group. Have one student read a question and then use it as a springboard to discuss the issues and rules of laws.

3. Read them to get a feel for your professor's style and to see what sort of topics the test might cover. Do the questions involve academic, philosophical issues? Or are they geared toward meat-and-potatoes knowledge? Are there curve balls? Are there multiple-choice or true-false questions as well as essay questions?

4. Finally, there always lurks the chance that a law student's greatest dream will come true: that Professor Jones didn't get around to thinking up a new fact pattern this year and has used the same exam he wrote two years ago—the very exam you spent three hours studying just last night. (Does this happen often? No. But in my years at school I took two entire exams that were very similar to past tests and several others that had questions modeled on previous ones.)

A word of warning: Old exams can be helpful, but not if you study them to the exclusion of your regular study regimen (read that master outline!). After all, it is this year's test, not last year's, that you've got to ace.

SLEEP—THE SECRET WEAPON

As you now know, the LCM system described in this book is a paced method of learning. It does not require a burst of energy at the end. In fact, you will ruin much of the work you've done during the semester and study week if you stay up late on the evening before the exam to cram.

If you've followed the LCM approach with reasonable diligence, there is absolutely no need for frantic, last-minute studying. You'll have a remarkable amount of information at your command. Spend the night before the exam calmly reading your master outline, memorizing your exam outline and answer format and—most important of all—getting a good night's sleep.

For a summary of the test-taking techniques in this chapter, please see Recap 3 on page 170.

Chapter Eleven

⚖ Taking Exams

[For a preview of this chapter,
see Recap 3 on p. 170]

You've studied for the exam. You wake up feeling somewhat like Lindbergh on the morning of his flight. You arrive at school two hours early (just in case you read the announced time incorrectly—six times). The proctors let you into the classroom, where you find your good-luck chair has been taken. You find another. You sit down.

Now what?

The first thing you have to do is the hardest part of the LCM system: Relax! Tell yourself: "I've done the classwork. I've written my outline. I've read it. I'm better prepared than most of my fellow students. Bring on the blue books!"

You calm down and begin going over the exam outline and answer format in your mind.

The proctor fires the starting gun, and your first law school exam is underway.

STEP ONE: READING THE INSTRUCTIONS

Before you do anything, rip apart an extra examination booklet or ask the proctor for some scrap paper. Place this in front of you. When the exam commences, read the instructions. *It is absolutely vital that you read them very carefully.*

The instructions may just say something like, "You have three hours in which to complete the exam." But they might contain some information that is necessary to remember as you answer the test questions. For instance, the professor might say, "In the following three exam questions, you are to assume you are in a state that adopts the majority rule in all the areas of law we have covered in class." Or: "Throughout the exam, you are the attorney representing the defendant." Or even: "Answer three of the following four questions."

Read these instructions first, and read them carefully.

STEP TWO: READING THE QUESTION

A typical law school exam asks you to resolve a legal conflict (most often reflected in a lawsuit or criminal trial, although sometimes in a business transaction). Therefore, in reading the question you need to mark three things:

- Who are the relevant parties? Identify each as the plaintiff, defendant, judge, bystander, or Mr. Red Herring. Circle these (circling makes for a less cluttered page than underlining).

- What are the issues (the legal questions you will have to answer in resolving the conflict) and what facts give rise to these issues? (This is where memorizing the exam outline will be most helpful. As you read the question, you will automatically test the facts against your mental image of the topics in the outline and the legal issues you have to address will emerge.) Circle these, and in the margin nearby jot a shorthand note indicating what the issues are.

- Are there pivot words? These are words like "not," "but," "although," "however," "and," and "or." These words are easily missed but might mean a difference in the outcome because they can change the meaning of a sentence dramatically. Again, circle these words.

Read the question once quickly, marking as mentioned above. Don't rewrite the question in the margin (there is a strong tendency to do this) and don't outline it. When you've finished the first reading, you're going to be tempted to start writing immediately. But don't. Go back and read it again.

Later in this book I'll give you some examples of what actual law school exams are like. However, I think it might be helpful here to take a look at an extremely simple example, one I'll refer to in this chapter as I go through the process of analyzing it.

Here is a mini exam question from contracts class.

Question One

Dave Dealer went to his door one day and found a package had been mistakenly delivered to his doorstep. He opened it up and found to his shock that it contained a kilo of marijuana. "This is terrible!" he said. "I should call the police." What he did, however, was to call his friend Peter Piper and said, "Hey, Peter, I just happen to have my paws on a stash of Des Moines gold. I'll sell it to you for a thousand bucks."

"Let me think about it," Peter said, fearing the phone line was tapped. After he hung up he sent Dave a note by messenger, saying, "You bet. You got a deal."

Dave, however, having watched a rerun of "Dragnet" in the meantime, had a change of heart and decided not to sell the drug after all. He sent a fax to Peter saying the deal was off. Dave received the note from the messenger at 10 A.M. and Peter received the fax at 10:01 A.M.

Peter offers the money to Dave and demands the dope. Peter claims a valid contract was made, and Dave says he effectively withdrew his offer. Peter sues Dave.

You're the judge. What's the outcome of the case?

STEP THREE: OUTLINING THE ANSWER

When you have finished the second reading, take the scrap paper and outline the answer. Never write an answer until you've outlined it. This outline should not be long—no more than a short list of the issues. Under each issue note the facts relevant to resolving it. In our contracts exam:

1. *Was K[1] formed?*
   —D made offer on phone
   —Pl sent messgr: I accept
   —D changed mind, sent fax
   —Pl rec'd fax
   —D rec'd messg
2. *If formed was K enforceable?*
   —subject matter illegal, drugs

STEP FOUR: WRITING THE ANSWER

After you've finished this brief outline, you'll write the answer itself. Print if you can't write neatly. I'd like to think professors are above taking off points for sloppiness, but they're human too. Remember that while you're home relaxing on holiday break they'll be plowing through 200 blue books. I suggest you take the extra effort to make their task easier. It certainly can't hurt.

The structure of each answer is the five-point answer format described at the end of the previous chapter (short-answer, issues presented, analysis, other considerations, and conclusion). The following describes what you will write in your answer under each of the five-part headings:

[Short Answer]

You shouldn't write anything in this space until you have completed the rest of the answer. Write the Roman numeral and leave a two- or three-line space then move on to the issues presented section. Why? Because you don't know what the short answer is yet. You may think you do, having outlined the answer and seen all the issues. But as you write your analysis section, you might change your mind. In fact, you might change your mind two or three times. By not writing your

---

[1] You should use abbreviations in this outline (K, remember, is the abbreviation for contract). Ask your professor before the test what abbreviations are acceptable to use in your answer.

short answer yet, you avoid having to cross out an incorrect response. Maintain the appearance of certainty.

When you have completed the analysis, return to this section and fill in the short answer. This should be a direct response to the question the professor has asked. This is important. If the question is whether the court should grant a judgment for the plaintiff or for the defendant, don't write, "The contract is enforceable." Say, rather: "The defendant will prevail."

You might be tempted to equivocate—a natural reflex of attorneys. Yet try to keep the qualifications to a minimum. It's better to say up front, "Yes, the plaintiff will win," and then demonstrate in your analysis section the various merits of both parties' contentions than to say, "The plaintiff will probably win, but the defendant has a good chance of winning also." Remember, in practice, lawyers are asked to give clear, definitive answers, and it is the mark of a good lawyer—and a successful student—to give unhesitant legal opinions. As Oliver Wendall Holmes, Jr., said, the law is predicting what a court will do.

Assuming you have completed the analysis (as I'll do in a moment) you would return to the short answer section of the contract question and write the following:

I. The outcome of the case is that Peter will lose.

Issues Presented

This section will state the questions of law that must be answered before you can reach your conclusion. This section is very important for two reasons.

First, your professor is testing you on your ability to find the issues in complex fact patterns as much as on your knowledge of the rules of law. By indicating the key issues at the beginning of your question, you'll let your professor know that you've already done half the job. Moreover, a clear statement of the issues will put the professor in a frame of mind favorable to your answer even before the analytical portions of your blue book are read.

Second, if you run short of time, you'll at least let your professor know that you've identified the issues; you'll get some, perhaps a great deal of, credit for an uncompleted answer.

When you write this section, you should assume your professor knows nothing of the law. State your issues as broadly as possible, then focus on the specific issue in the question. An overall issue in the law of contracts is: "Was there offer and acceptance?" Well, this is a correct statement of a legal problem. But it's not *as* correct as focusing on the portion of the issue that's reflected in the fact pattern. For instance: "Was there offer and acceptance (specifically, was the oral offer properly revoked by A before B accepted it)?"

In our contracts exam:

II. *Issues presented:*
    A. *Was a contract formed?*
        1. *Was there proper offer and acceptance?*
        2. *Was the offer revoked before acceptance by Peter?*
    B. *If a contract was formed, did the subject matter render it illegal and thus unenforceable?*

Analysis

The analysis portion of the exam answer is the three-step approach from the exam answer format:

- Rule of law
- Applicable facts
- Conclusion

Each issue should be handled separately and marked with its own subhead, like "Issue A" or "Issue 1." There is no need to restate the issue because it will be just inches above.

Below this heading, write in textual form the general rule of law that is applicable to this situation and any exceptions or subrules that might apply.

Following this, put a *very* brief reference to the facts that you are applying the rule to. For instance, in our contracts example:

III. Analysis

    A. Was a contract made?

The elements of a contract are (1) offer and acceptance, (2) consideration, and (3) capacity of the parties.

Here, it is clear that there is consideration (the money exchanged for the drugs), and we have no reason from the facts to believe that Dave or Peter were underage or otherwise lacked the capacity to enter into a contract. However, there is an issue as to whether there was an offer and acceptance.

The traditional rule is that an offer must be accepted by the same means by which it was made.

Here, Dave would argue that Peter sent the acceptance by another means than telephone, so that it was not effective.

However, the modern rule is that if some different method of acceptance is used, the offer will nevertheless be deemed accepted and thus a contract will be formed as long as the acceptance is actually received by the offeror.

Here, the court would probably follow this modern rule and hold that the means of acceptance was okay because Dave actually received it.

The second issue is whether Dave effectively revoked his offer before Peter accepted. The majority rule is that an offer to a contract may be revoked at any time prior to its acceptance. Again, the majority rule is that if sent by a means other than the acceptance, it is effective upon receipt.

Here, Dave received Peter's acceptance before Peter received Dave's revocation. Therefore, there was offer and acceptance.

    B. Was the contract illegal and thus unenforceable?

Another element of a valid contract is legality. The rule is that a contract is illegal if, according to the Restatement of Contracts, its formation or performance is criminal, tortious, or otherwise opposed to public policy.

In certain instances (if, for instance, one of the parties is ignorant of the law or if there is a statute to protect one of the parties—such as securities law statutes) an illegal contract may be enforceable, but none of those exceptions apply here.

The purchase and sale of drugs are clearly within this category. Therefore, the contract would be unenforceable by Peter.

Other Considerations

Once you have completed the legal reasoning portion of the question, it is time to turn to the extra credit portion of your answer. Here you will present a brief discussion of the material that appeared last in your master outline—the miscellaneous material including public policy issues, some views presented by your professor, some bit of sociology or legal philosophy you find relevant or interesting.

Keep it short and make sure the comments you have are appropriate. Don't bring in irrelevant information. Remember that this is *extra* credit. Forget about this section if you don't have enough time to answer other questions, or if you don't have anything meaningful to add to your answer.

IV. Other considerations

As Professor Jones writes in her famous article, there are strong public policy reasons for enforcing some illegal contracts, particularly if it appears as if one party is using the traditional rule to take advantage of the other party. Peter's lawyer would be unable to successfully make such an argument, however, because of the competing social interest in limiting the sale and use of drugs.

Conclusion

The conclusion is a very brief statement to the effect that, based on your legal analysis of all the issues and other considerations matters, the dispute should be answered this way or that. It is here that you will weigh the answers of the various issues and decide in favor of one party or the other. This section is a formality and should contain no independent reasoning of its own.

The conclusion tidies things up nicely and is the final part of the formal legal reasoning process, but because your answer will be found in the other parts of the blue book (the

short answer and the rule/analysis sections), you can eliminate the conclusion if you find yourself in a bind for time.

V. Conclusion

*Therefore, although a contract was in fact formed between
Dave and Peter, it would be unenforceable because it was an
illegal contract. There are no public policy issues to dictate a
different conclusion.*

Finally, after you have finished with the conclusion section,
don't forget to go back and write the short answer response.
Here are all the elements of the exam in order:

CONTRACTS I EXAM

Question One

I. The outcome of the case is that Peter will lose.
II. Issues presented:
   A. Was a contract formed?
     1. Was there proper offer and acceptance?
     2. Was the offer revoked before acceptance by Peter?
   *B. If a contract was formed, did the subject matter
     render it illegal and thus unenforceable?*
III. Analysis
   A. Was a contract made?

*The elements of a contract are (1) offer and acceptance, (2)
consideration, and (3) capacity of the parties.*
   *Here, it is clear that there is consideration (the money ex-
changed for the drugs), and we have no reason from the facts
to believe that Dave or Peter were underage or otherwise
lacked the capacity to enter into a contract. However, there is
an issue as to whether there was an offer and acceptance.*
   *The traditional rule is that an offer must be accepted by
the same means by which it was made.*
   *Here, Dave would argue that Peter sent the acceptance by
another means than telephone, so that it was not effective.*
   *However, the modern rule is that if some different method
of acceptance is used, the offer will nevertheless be deemed*

accepted and thus a contract will be formed as long as the acceptance is actually received by the offeror.

Here, the court would probably follow this modern rule and hold that the means of acceptance was okay because Dave actually received it.

The second issue is whether Dave effectively revoked his offer before Peter accepted. The majority rule is that an offer to a contract may be revoked at any time prior to its acceptance. Again, the majority rule is that if sent by a means other than the acceptance, it is effective upon receipt.

Here, Dave received Peter's acceptance before Peter received Dave's revocation. Therefore, there was offer and acceptance.

B. Was the contract illegal and thus unenforceable?

Another element of a valid contract is legality. The rule is that a contract is illegal if, according to the Restatement of Contracts, its formation or performance is criminal, tortious, or otherwise opposed to public policy.

In certain instances (if, for instance, one of the parties is ignorant of the law or if there is a statute to protect one of the parties—such as securities law statutes—an illegal contract may be enforceable, but none of those exceptions apply here.

The purchase and sale of drugs are clearly within this category. Therefore, the contract would be unenforceable by Peter.

IV. Other considerations

As Professor Jones writes in her famous article, there are strong public policy reasons for enforcing some illegal contracts, particularly if it appears as if one party is using the traditional rule to take advantage of the other party. Peter's lawyer would be unable to successfully make such an argument, however, because of the competing social interest in limiting the sale and use of drugs.

V. Conclusion

Therefore, although a contract was in fact formed between Dave and Peter, it would be unenforceable because it was an illegal contract. There are no public policy issues to dictate a different conclusion.

Keeping the Players Straight

Each law school essay exam question will involve a complex fact pattern giving rise to at least several lawsuits: *A* v. *B, B* v. *A, B* v. *C,* and so on. You should view each suit as a separate question. The five-part answer format will be used to resolve each suit. For instance:

Question I

A v. *B*

    I. [Short answer]
   II. Issues presented
  III. Analysis
      Issue 1
        [Rule of law]
        [Applicable facts]
        [Conclusion]
      Issue 2
        [Rule of law]
        [Applicable facts]
        [Conclusion]
  IV. Other considerations
   V. Conclusion

B v. *A*

    I. [Short answer]
   II. Issues presented
  III. Analysis
      Issue 1
        [Rule of law]
        [Applicable facts]
        [Conclusion]
      Issue 2
        [Rule of law]
        [Applicable facts]
        [Conclusion]
  IV. Other considerations
   V. Conclusion

Note that even if the fact pattern involves only two parties, the professor will include different, maybe many, causes of action. It is common in real-life lawsuits for the parties to sue each other for all their grievances whether the complaints are related or not. For instance, if A has been libeled by B and, coincidentally, A runs into B's car, the parties may combine into a single lawsuit A's suit against B for the libel and B's suit against A for damage to the car. (These are called different "causes of action.")

Therefore, in your exam, you will have to clearly differentiate the various causes of action:

Question II

    A v. *B* on libel claim
       I. [Short answer]
      II. Issues presented
     III. Analysis
         Issue 1
           [Rule of law]
           [Applicable facts]
           [Conclusion]
         Issue 2
           [Rule of law]
           [Applicable facts]
           [Conclusion]
     IV. Other considerations
      V. Conclusion

    B v. *A* on auto negligence claim
       I. [Short answer]
      II. Issues presented
     III. Analysis
         Issue 1
           [Rule of law]
           [Applicable facts]
           [Conclusion]
         Issue 2
           [Rule of law]
           [Applicable facts]
           [Conclusion]
     IV. Other considerations
      V. Conclusion

BUDGETING TIME

You should allocate a certain block of time for each question, depending on the point value assigned to it by the professor. Spend up to half of that time reading and analyzing the question and outlining it before you begin writing the answer.

You should regard the end of the time block as a Cinderella deadline—pumpkin time and bad news if you don't leave that question and move on to the next one. Obviously, you must remain somewhat flexible, but it is far better to answer all questions in as much depth as time allows rather than to answer one or two in great depth and be unable to answer the last question.

If you do run short of time and are unable to do more than just scratch the surface of the last question because you have devoted so much time to the earlier ones, write a short note to your professor to that effect. If your early answers evidence your knowledge of the material and skills in legal analysis, your professor will probably understand that your failure to answer is indeed lack of time and not uncertainty as to the substance of the law. The professor might take this into consideration in giving you points for the unfinished answer.

However you use your time, always leave at least five minutes to reread as much of the answer as you can. This is to clean up punctuation, to make sure that you didn't write "plaintiff" when you meant "defendant," and so on.

EMERGENCIES

No matter how prepared you are, emergencies sometimes happen. You may have gotten stymied on the first two questions and have only ten minutes left in which to answer the last one. Your watch breaks and you lose track of the time. Or, more likely, you simply panic and your mind goes blank. In any event, you don't have either the time or the ability to analyze the fact pattern and write an answer according to the LCM system.

What are you going to do?

Use the exam outline as a parachute.

In your blue book, write an exam outline topic heading that seems to have something to do with the facts. Beneath this, write the rule of law for that topic, throw in some facts, and draw a conclusion. Go on to the next exam outline topic heading and do the same, for so long as you have time remaining. Don't worry about correctly analyzing the factual situation in the question. Concentrate on getting as much information from your brain onto the paper as you can. Show your professor that although you perhaps aren't responding directly to the question, you know a massive amount of law.

A true story: I used the LCM approach to study for exams in all my courses, including the upper-class course of corporate taxation. I went into the exam comfortably prepared, sat down, turned over the question sheet, and froze in horror. There was a single question, one or two sentences long. No matter how many times I read it, the question seemed to have nothing to do with anything I'd learned in the course. I spent probably half the exam period in a panic, trying to figure out what the professor wanted us to do.

I finally gave up on the fact pattern and poured out my exam outline, added the rules of law and statutory citations (from the Internal Revenue Code and related regulations), and then threw in at the end of each topic a lame sentence like, "Therefore Jones might want to issue stock because he could do so in a tax-free exchange."

I left the test believing in my heart I had failed the course. (And it was no reassurance to me that half the class felt the same way.) I went on to other tests, resigned that although I sure didn't want the black mark of a failing grade on my record, at least I had some extra course credits and would not need the two hours of corporate taxation to graduate.

When the grades were posted, a month later, I went reluctantly to the bulletin board to see how badly I'd done. I found my anonymous student number. I looked next to it for the grade. The number was circled—my school's way of indicating the highest grade in the class (true, it was a 92—an A minus). To this day I couldn't tell you what the professor was looking for; but I do know the exam outline saved my life.

HOW TO GET AN A FOR A WRONG ANSWER

I want to offer some reassurance here. You are not a lawyer; you're a law student. Although you will have learned a great deal over the course of your semester, in taking your exams you will not be held to the same standard as a practicing attorney or a judge. It is entirely conceivable that you will walk out of the exam and return home to realize that you got the answer dead wrong.

Maybe you missed a fact or interpreted a phrase wrong, or maybe you mistook the plaintiff for the defendant.

Don't drop out yet.

Law school is not like undergraduate school. While they may not admit it, law professors want correct legal reasoning skills—not correct results. How can you have one but not the other? Easily. Professors understand the kind of pressure you're under and know how simple it is to miss facts or mix up rules. If you successfully identify the issues, and state the applicable rule of law, you have done 90 percent of the required work. Even if you let a wrongdoer off the hook or sock an innocent bystander with a huge judgment, you still might get the A you deserve.

CURVE BALLS

The scene: You've done your outline. You've read it until you know every smudge on every page. You've memorized your exam outline. You know the answer format. You've grammatically diagrammed every sentence of your professor's past exams for the last three years, all of which have been long fact patterns. You are, in short, prepared.

You sit down in the examination room. Why, there's hardly room for both you and your confidence in the same chair! You turn over the question sheet, your mind running through the exam outline; you're ready to pile up issues like slicing salami.

You look at the question. The entire exam, not just the first question, but the *entire exam,* reads as follows.

According to Lewis Carroll's Father William:
"In my youth," said his father, "I took to the law
And argued each case with my wife;
And the muscular strength, which it gave to my jaws,
Has lasted the rest of my life."
Discuss all implications as they relate to civil procedure.
Mr. Carroll may have been English, but you should be con-
cerned solely with American law. Post-1938, of course.

Wait! Stay conscious. You'll be a lawyer yet.

This happens occasionally. Maybe the thought of writing yet another fact pattern has pushed the professor over the brink. The result is one of those rare exams with no fact pattern, no apparent relationship to anything you have learned, maybe no apparent relationship to law at all. Poetry. Quotes from popular novels. Fairy tales.

What do you do? There are three things to remember:

1. Don't panic. If you're prepared for a typical essay exam, you are equally prepared for this anomaly.

2. Figure out if the professor is trying to get at something specific. Is there perhaps some particular inquiry in mind? It may be that your professor is really asking a straightforward question that is simply disguised. Take a few minutes to figure out if this is what's happening. If so, organize your answer as you would a typical undergraduate essay and write away.[2]

In the Lewis Carroll example, for instance, you could properly deduce that the professor is interested in the oral argument process. Reference also is made to 1938, the year the Federal Rules of Civil Procedure, with their simplified approach to procedure in federal courts, became operative. It's a

---

[2] For instance, I heard of a civil procedure professor whose exam—or at least one question on it—consisted solely of lyrics from Beatles' songs. There didn't seem to be any relation among the songs themselves, let alone to civil procedure. On second reading, though, the professor's question emerged: Each line related in some way to a stage in the pleading process. The list of random lyrics was not random at all, but a lawsuit in verse. Simply stating the rules applicable to each stage of pleading was what the professor wanted.

fair guess that the professor is asking about the pleading process—the series of documents that pass between the parties to get a lawsuit off the ground. At one time, much of the pleading was oral and later, even when written, was very complicated and exasperatingly formal, requiring great "strength of jaw," figuratively, if not literally. Your answer, then, would be a discussion of the pleading rules in federal court and how the post-1938 scheme has been simplified.

Exactly what does this professor want? Who knows? But it's a reasonable approach for you to take, and if you do a thorough job, you'll get a good grade.

3. If you simply cannot find any hidden question or specific inquiry, use the shotgun approach. The question may be bizarre and it may be unlegal, but remember that your professors haven't been sweating away all year to teach you bizarre, unlegal rules. They've taught you very specific rules of law and how to apply them. Show them what you've learned.

Find some transition, some premises or observation that ties the subject of law to a specific aspect of the quotation or question you have been given. Once you have done that, give them both barrels. Mentally scan your exam outline and spend the rest of the exam period writing an essay that incorporates every aspect of law you've studied that semester if it in any way relates to the supposed theme.

CROSS-REFERENCING

Don't assume your professor will refer back to material in one of your prior questions. For instance, in question 3, you might state simply "Because of the parol evidence rule, the answer is that the D will win," without mentioning what that rule is because you have just described it fully in question 2. But unless you're so strapped for time that it's impossible for you to write out the rule, you should repeat it, or at least say, "Because of the parol evidence rule (see the discussion in question 2), the answer is that the D will win."

Professors often don't read each student's book from cover

to cover. Instead, they read everyone's first question, grade them, then turn to the second, and so on. This helps in arriving at a grading standard. To eliminate your losing points for appearing not to know the answer and to eliminate professors' headaches (having to rifle back through your earlier answers), try to make each response self-contained.

If, however, there are several causes of action within a single question, then cross-referencing is a necessity. For instance, if the question has two lawsuits in it—*A* v. *B* for negligence and *B* v. *C* for negligence—do a complete job on the *A* v. *B* portion of your answer, clearly stating all the applicable rules. When you turn to *B* v. *C*, you can at least refer back to the basic rules contained in the *A* v. *B* part of your answer even though the specific issues are bound to be somewhat different. This cross-referencing is illustrated in the sample exam answers in the next chapter.

SURVIVAL RATIONS

Some students like to bring candy and gum to an exam. If you want such things, fine, but don't distract yourself or others with edibles. I found that something cold to drink halfway through the test seemed to give me a nice burst of energy. You won't be allowed to smoke during the exam unless there is a separate smokers' section or exam room, but if you feel the urge so strongly that you become distracted, step out into the hall for three or four minutes for a cigarette.

CELEBRATE

When it's over with, no postmortems. Don't discuss the exam with classmates. Everyone will have found at least one issue no one else thought of and will gleefully point out the fact. Listening to such discussions will make you wonder if you took the same exam as everybody else.

If there is any way to avoid it, do not study for future exams on the night of one you've finished. You need relaxation more than input. Have some fun. Get some sleep.

For a summary of the test-taking techniques in this chapter, please see Recap 3 on page 170.

Chapter Twelve

⚖ Sample Exams

*[For a preview of this chapter,
see Recap 3 on p. 170.]*

$\mathbf{T}$his chapter presents two sample exams. As with the sample briefs in Chapter 6, we'll start out with a simple question—probably more simple than what you'll see in class—and then move on to a harder one. The first is from a contracts class; the second, from torts. Don't try to read the question and answer it. In fact, don't even pay much attention to what *my* answer to the question is. This book isn't meant to teach you contracts and torts; its goal is to familiarize you with law school exams and to teach you how to recognize issues and organize answers.

Contracts I   Examination

Zoe was walking down the main street of Alphaville in the State of Omega one nice day in June. He was pleased because he had just finished his last law school exam and was looking forward to a summer of relative relaxation as a ditchdigger.

He noticed in front of him a classmate, Dip. Zoe didn't care much for Dip because Dip had reneged on a loan Zoe had made him. Zoe had lent Dip $100 ten years before when Dip was still a minor and his promise to pay couldn't be enforced against him.

Suddenly, though, Zoe noticed a huge safe fall from a fire escape above Dip's head. Zoe acted quickly. He raced forward

---

and pushed Dip out of the way. The safe just missed both of them.

Dip was so grateful that he blurted out, "Zoe, you know that $100 I owe you? Well, I'm going to pay it back. Meet me tomorrow at my bank, and I'll give you the cash."

But, naturally, Dip didn't show up. It didn't matter anyhow because the safe that nearly fell on him was his bank's, and there was no money available for withdrawals. Subsequent attempts to get the money from Dip, however, have been in vain. His general response is a studied, "Huh?"

Zoe has walked into your law office and wants to sue Dip for the money. What is the claim, what are the colorable defenses, and who wins?

As you were reading the first time, you should have been circling:

- the parties
- those facts that are legally significant (and noting in the margin the issues those facts give rise to)
- pivot words ("but," "not," "however," etc.)

Once you finish reading, go back and read the material again, marking facts and issues you may have missed. A marked copy of the exam question, upon completion of two readings, might look like this:

CONTRACTS I EXAMINATION

Zoe was walking down the main street of Alphaville in the State of Omega one nice day in June. He was pleased because he had just

He's over 21   finished his last law school exam and was looking forward to a summer of relative relaxation as a ditchdigger.

He's over 21 too   He noticed in front of him a classmate, Dip. Zoe didn't care much for Dip because Dip had reneged on a loan Zoe had made him. Zoe

Unenforce. debt   had lent Dip $100 ten years before when Dip
Statute/limitat?   was still a minor and his promise to pay couldn't be enforced against him.

Suddenly, though, Zoe noticed a huge safe

Unrequested act

fall from a fire escape above Dip's head. Zoe acted quickly. He raced forward and pushed Dip out of the way. The safe just missed both of them.

Contract?
Oral promise
to pay old debt—
statute of frauds?

Dip was so grateful that he blurted out, "Zoe, you know that $100 I owe you? Well, I'm going to pay it back. Meet me tomorrow at my bank, and I'll give you the cash."

Breach

But, naturally, Dip didn't show up. It didn't matter anyhow because the safe that nearly fell on him was his bank's, and there was no money available for withdrawals. Subsequent attempts to get the money from Dip, however, have been in vain. His general response is a studied, "Huh?"

Zoe has walked into your law office and wants to sue Dip for the money. What is the claim, what are the colorable defenses, and who wins?

Mentally, you would now reduce the question to the essential, legally relevant facts.

- D owed Z money under prior unenforceable promise.
- Z performed an act for D, and then D orally promised to repay the debt.
- D breached.

The whole question comes down to these three points. You will have framed the issues very generally during your reading. Essentially they are in the areas of contract consideration, the statute of frauds, and the statute of limitations. Of course, if you start scribbling about consideration and the statutes right away, you're not doing a complete job. What is the specific question? A client wants an answer. So you start with the basics:

Is there a contract that can be enforced in court?

And specifically: How do consideration, the statute of limitations, and the statute of frauds affect the creation and enforceability of that contract?

On scratch paper you outline your answer in very brief terms.

    1. *Contract created?*
    Consideration problem
       Past consideration—good defense
       Reaffirming prior promise—not good defense
    2. *Statute of frauds—writing not necessary*
    3. *Statute of limitations—suit okay, statute runs from time of second promise*

Now you are ready to write the answer:

  I. *Zoe will be able to sue Dip for breach of contract and recover the $100.*
 II. *Issues*
    1. *Are the elements of a contract present?*
      a. Is consideration absent because Zoe's act is past consideration?
      b. Is the consideration substitute of reaffirming a prior promise sufficient?
    2. *Is the statute of frauds a valid defense?*
    3. *Is the statute of limitations a valid defense?*
III. *Analysis*

Issue 1.
Zoe would sue Dip for breach of contract. In order to do so, a plaintiff must show an enforceable contract exists. The elements of such a contract are agreement (i.e., mutual assent through offer and acceptance), consideration, capacity, and legality. The facts indicate there was an agreement and capacity (they were in law school; thus over 21), and even if the earlier promise might in some way have been illegal, there is nothing wrong with the second promise.

But there is a consideration problem. A promise is not enforceable unless supported by some consideration, that is, a benefit to the promisor or detriment to the promisee. It is the majority rule, though, that a promise supported by past consideration is not enforceable because the promise did not induce the act. Here the consideration for Dip's promise was Zoe's saving him. But Zoe's good deed occurred before the promise; it was thus past consideration.

A few courts accept the promissory restitution doctrine, which imposes a moral obligation to pay for benefits received. But this is the minority view. Similarly, some states might allow recovery under the rules of quasi-contracts, in which an obligation to repay the reasonable value of services rendered will be implied. Yet this doctrine usually applies only when commercial-type services have been rendered (repairs, painting, etc.), not in situations like that presented.

However, there are exceptions to the general requirement of consideration. They include the old concept of sealed contracts, modifications under the Uniform Commercial Code (UCC), and others. One of these is the rule that when one promises to pay a debt that is presently unenforceable because of one party's infancy or other operation of law, the promise will be valid without consideration.

Here Dip's promise as a teenager is unenforceable because it was made when he had no capacity to contract and because it is barred by operation of law (the statute of limitations). Thus, his new promise to repay (called "ratification") is fully enforceable without consideration.

Issue 2.

Dip would raise the defense of the statute of frauds, which states that some contracts will not be enforceable unless in writing and signed by the party to be charged. However, not all contracts are within the rule. The main ones are those to pay the debts of another, real property transactions, and contracts not capable of being performed in one year. Here, Dip's promise does not fall into any of these categories. Therefore his oral promise is binding.

Issue 3.

Dip might also argue that the statute of limitations would bar the suit by Zoe. This rule provides that if suit is not brought within (usually) six years of the breach, the plaintiff cannot sue. Dip would argue that the original breach, which occurred more than ten years ago, should be the measuring date. However, courts in situations like this one look to the second breach. Thus Zoe will have six years from the date of the second breach in which to sue for Dip's recent promise to repay.

[There are no "other considerations" here, so don't waste

your time and the professor's trying to make some up. Go to the next question—or to the local tavern.]

IV. Conclusion

Dip's promise is a valid contract and enforceable without consideration because of the consideration substitute mentioned earlier. Further, there are no defenses under the statute of frauds or statute of limitations.

Torts II Examination
(Allow 2½ Hours)

One pleasant day in September, Sam was driving his 1966 Chevy, which had never undergone a safety inspection, down I-70 in the State of Zed, which follows the majority, common-law rules of tort law and has no relevant statutes, except as noted.

Sam pulled over to pick up Hank, a student hitchhiking his way to college. Although he appeared to be 18 or 19, in fact he was only 17, having skipped a grade some ten years before. The age of capacity in Zed is 18. Sam told Hank he could have a ride if he wanted to chance it, but the old car "just ain't what she used to be" and had been known to lose wheels at inopportune moments. Hank shrugged and got in the car.

As they drove along at a speed higher than that posted (a speed that Hank noticed, but did not comment upon), Hank observed a cow flying along beside them. He casually called Sam's attention to the fact. Sure enough, there was a cow! It was slung beneath a helicopter being transported from one field to another. Watching the cow, Sam ran the car off the road into a compost heap, injuring hank and destroying the car. Albert, a farmer standing atop the compost, was not harmed.

The noise from the collision so alarmed the cow that she squirmed violently and slipped from the sling, which had been made by the Acme Cow Sling Company, Inc. The cow fell to the ground, and although she was unharmed, landed on three hens, sending them directly to the Great Chicken Coop in the Sky. The sling, it turned out, had been made under conditions of the utmost quality control and inspection and had been properly strapped around the cow by the pilot. Nevertheless, a cow sling expert hired by Albert testified that a properly made sling would not have allowed the cow to fall. His testimony has not been disputed by Acme or anyone else. Albert and his wife, Sally, owned the late chickens and the cow.

When Sally learned the tragic news of the deaths of her prize hen, Poulet, and Poulet's sisters, she suffered an anxiety attack, developed insomnia that lasted for several days, and could not bring herself to make omelets for the better part of a month.

You are the law clerk to the judge in Onawananoga County, where the various lawsuits arising out of the events have been filed. They are the following:

1. Hank v. Sam for personal injury.

2. Albert v. Sam for property damage (for the chickens only; the compost was still usable).

3. Sally v. Acme for her distraught state.

Please prepare a memorandum for the judge, discussing what causes of action exist, the defenses thereto, and who will prevail and why. But please do so briefly; the judge is also county fire marshal and owner of the local general store and doesn't have much time for such silly litigation.

HANK v. SAM

I. Hank will prevail in an action against Sam for negligence.

II. Issues

1. Was Sam negligent with respect to Hank?

2. Did Hank assume the risk of harm because of what Sam said to him?

3. Did Hank and Sam enter an exculpatory agreement based on what Sam said to Hank?

4. Was Hank contributorily negligent?

III. Analysis

1. A prima facie case of negligence is made out upon a showing of a duty owed by the defendant to the plaintiff, a breach of that duty, a causal relation between the breach and the harm, and damages.

A duty exists if it is foreseeable that harm would occur to someone if the defendant didn't exercise the care of a reasonably prudent person. Here it was obviously foreseeable to Sam that Hank could be harmed if he weren't careful. So there was a duty on Sam's part.

A breach of that duty occurs when the defendant does not meet the standard of care of a reasonably prudent person, an objective level of conduct. In Judge Hand's approach (used by courts in deciding if the jury correctly found a breach), a breach occurs when the likelihood and severity of a harm outweigh the burden of precautions. Here Sam breached his duty by speeding and watching the cow when he should have been more careful. Note that although the car had not been inspected for safety, that appears to be irrelevant because there is no causal relation between the failure to have an inspection and the accident.

Causation is a two-step analysis. First, is there cause in fact? That is, would the plaintiff's harm have occurred but for the defendant's act? Here, that test is met. Second, was there proximate cause? This asks the court to decide whether—once it has been shown that the defendant's act was a cause in fact of the harm—the law wishes him to be liable for the harm. There are two tests for proximate cause: the foreseeable risk test (proximate cause is found only if the harm was a foreseeable consequence of the defendant's act), known as the Palsgraf rule, and the direct consequence, or liability-beyond-risk test (proximate cause is found if the harm, even if unforeseeable, is a direct consequence of the defendant's action). Under either of these tests, Sam's conduct would clearly have been the proximate cause of Hank's harm.

Damages require some harm more than nominal damages, such as might be recovered in a suit for battery or assault. Here, Hank's personal injury is sufficient to qualify for damages. Thus, a claim for negligence exists.

2. Generally, a plaintiff will be barred from recovery if he assumes a risk—that is, if with actual knowledge that he might be harmed, proceeds anyway to risk getting hurt. Sam would assert that Hank knew of the risk of driving with him because of what Sam told Hank about the car, that is, the wheels' falling off.

However, the risk that actually existed was Sam's carelessness as a driver, not the condition of the car, so Hank could not be said to have assumed a known risk.

3. A plaintiff can agree to waive a claim for negligence against someone else prior to the time an injury occurs. These "exculpatory agreements," however, are actual contracts and aren't enforceable unless all the requirements for a valid contract exist. Here Hank was below the age of capacity to enter a valid contract. Moreover, courts show great dislike for these agreements; a casual statement by Sam would not be enforced against an injured teenager.

4. A plaintiff's own negligence will completely bar recovery in those states that do not have a new comparative fault rule. Zed appears to have the old contributory negligence rule, under which Hank would be barred from recovery if Sam could show he was negligent in failing to point out the speed of the car and in calling Sam's attention to the cow.

Note that Hank's age would not be a defense to any claim for negligence; an infant can be liable for negligence although the standard of liability may be different than that for an adult.

However, neither of these activities seems so serious a breach as to fall below the standard of a reasonably prudent person; it's not as if Hank grabbed the wheel or covered Sam's eyes while he drove.

IV. Other considerations

Additionally, Hank would have a strong tactical advantage. In this cause of action, the major issue is breach of duty, which is a question for the jury (as are the cause and damages issues). If we assume that Hank is a clean-cut, hard-working college student, his attorney would request a jury—which would probably resolve the breach issue in Hank's favor.

V. Conclusion

Hank would have a negligence action against Sam for per-

sonal injury. The defenses that might be raised by Sam would not be successful, and Hank would recover.

ALBERT v. SAM

I. Albert could recover against Sam for property damage in an action for negligence.

II. Issue

Was Sam negligent with respect to Albert, or was the flying cow a superseding cause?

III. Analysis

The same rule of negligence described earlier—in the case above—controls the suit by Albert. Here the duty issue is questionable, but it could be reasonably asserted that Sam owed a duty to Albert, who might in some way be harmed by Sam's action. Further, driving a speeding car off the road was probably a breach of this duty. As to damages, property damage is properly a wrong for which the plaintiff can recover in a negligence suit.

The causation issue presents a problem, however. If Sam had run over the chickens, there would be no problem. But because the chain of events resulting in the cow's fall onto the chickens involves several steps, the issue isn't clear.

As to cause in fact, Sam's negligence satisfies that requirement. But for his hitting the compost, the cow would not have squirmed and fallen.

As to proximate cause, however, Sam would argue that (1) the harm was not a foreseeable consequence of his negligence and (2) that the defective cow sling was a superseding cause that relieved Sam of liability.

Under the proximate cause rule stated earlier, the direct causation rule would allow Sam to be found liable. Moreover, under the majority foreseeable risk rule, it is possible that this conduct would be considered to have resulted in foreseeable harms (injury to farm animals) even if the actual consequences were not foreseeable (squashed chickens).

In light of the authority of Kinsman Transit and Wagon Mound 2, which represent a move away from the strict Pals-

graf approach, it is likely that Sam's conduct would be the proximate cause of the loss of the chickens.

With respect to the superseding cause argument, the rule as to superseding causes is that an actor will not be liable for his negligence if the plaintiff's harm results from an intervening cause (a cause of the harm arising after the defendant's negligence) that is unforeseeable—thus becoming a "superseding" cause (the sling in this case, Sam would argue). However, Sam could not win this argument, for the defect in the sling existed prior to the time of Sam's negligence. Thus, the defect could not be an intervening, superseding cause. Rather, the sling maker and Sam would be concurrent tortfeasors, and Albert would be free to sue either or both. Sam will not be relieved from liability by virtue of the defective sling.

IV. Conclusion

Because there was no superseding cause, Sam would be liable to Albert for property damage as a result of Sam's negligence.

SALLY v. ACME

I. Sally would probably not be able to recover for her emotional distress.

II. Issues

1. Would Sally have a cause of action for negligence against Acme?

2. Would Sally have a cause of action for strict products liability against Acme?

3. Would Sally be able to recover emotional distress damages?

III. Analysis

1. As indicated earlier, the rule as to negligence requires that the defendant fall below the standard of care of a reasonably prudent person before liability will be found. It does not appear that Acme did so; its inspection processes and quality control indicate that it took great care. Thus, it was not negligent.

Note, however, that the fact that Sally was not in privity (contractual relationship) with Acme would not defeat her claim. Under the MacPherson decision, a plaintiff injured by a defective product need not show she had bought the product from the defendant. Nonetheless, Sally could not win owing to the lack of negligence on Acme's part.

2. As to strict products liability, the rule is that a seller will be liable for all harm (personal injury or property damage) caused by a product that is defective and unreasonably dangerous when it leaves the seller's control even though the seller exercised all due care and was not negligent in putting out the product provided the seller is in the business of selling. Restatement (2d) of Torts Section 402A.

The rule is an attempt to avoid the proof problems that injured consumers faced when suing manufacturers when those manufacturers were not negligent, but nonetheless sold a defective product. Strict products liability also stems from an effort to shift losses back to manufacturing companies, which are in a better position to bear the cost of the harm than individuals.

As with negligence, privity is not required between the plaintiff and the defendant in order to sue.

Here if it is established that the sling was defective when it left the control of Acme, which is presumably in the business of selling slings, Sally would properly have a cause of action in strict products liability. Acme, as seller, was under a duty not to sell a defective sling; it breached that duty, and Sally was harmed as a result.

3. Damages for emotional distress sought in either negligence or strict products liability suits may be awarded only in limited circumstances because courts wish to avoid fake claims and imposing too great a liability on defendants. If the tortfeasor actually hurts the plaintiff (if the cow had fallen on Sally), then she could recover emotional distress damages. If not, then the emotional shock must result in some physical manifestation of harm—nervousness, sleeplessness, illness, and the like. This did happen to Sally although not very serious harms developed.

However, there is an additional requirement when the tortfeasor's conduct does not result in injury to the plaintiff. Courts require something more than just emotional distress harm. The majority rule is that a plaintiff can recover only if the plaintiff was in the "zone of danger" when the harm occurred. Thus, if a mother is nearly hit by a car that does strike and kill her child, the emotional distress she experiences because of her child's death can be recoverable.

Here, however, it does not appear that Sally was in the zone of danger under the falling cow. Thus, it is unlikely that she would recover. Moreover, most of the cases allowing recovery have involved witnessing deaths of, or injury to, close family members; the death of pet chickens seems a bit weak to support a claim for emotional distress.

IV. *Other Considerations*

Although the analysis of this cause of action speaks in terms of emotional distress "damages," the context is actually a duty issue. Does the seller have a duty to protect a person from emotional distress?

A duty issue is to be resolved by the court. Here the court will have to consider conflicting policies. On the one hand, strict products liability arose to protect injured consumers who had no other redress against manufacturers. The rules recently have been very liberally construed to favor such consumers—so much so that some courts are beginning to worry about the economic impact on manufacturing in this country caused by the volume of products liability litigation.

On the other hand, this is not the traditional sort of harm that strict products liability was meant to remedy. As indicated in the Greenman v. Yuba Power Products case, the purpose of the cause of action is to help seriously injured consumers who would otherwise be without any remedy. Here, Sally (or Albert) could recover for the loss of the chickens, but her emotional harm was not serious, and it is therefore doubtful that she would prevail.

V. *Conclusion*

Although Sally would in theory have a cause of action for

strict products liability, she would not be able to recover for her emotional distress because she was not in the zone of danger.

Recap 3   Preparing For and Taking Exams
Studying for the Exam

1. Read and reread your master outline until you know the rule upon glancing at the heading. Do not memorize the outline.

2. Make an exam outline, covering the general topics you will be responsible for on the exam, in the order in which you feel they should be addressed. This should be no more than one or two pages in length. Memorize it.

3. Learn this or a similar answer format you will follow in answering your questions:

  I. [Short answer]
 II. Issues presented
III. Analysis
         First issue
         Second issue
         Final issue
 IV. Other considerations
  V. Conclusion

4. Get plenty of sleep the night before the exam.

Taking the Exam

1. Read the instructions.

2. Read the question twice, visualizing the facts. Circle key events, people, and pivot words. Take notes in the margin about issues you spot.

3. Outline the answer on scratch paper in very brief phrases. Do not rewrite the question.

4. Write your answer according to the answer format you have determined. When you begin, leave the short answer section blank. Take a definite stand. Don't restate the question. Be succinct. When you've finished with

the analysis, show off a little in the other considerations section of your answer. When you have finished, go back and provide a response in the short answer section.

5. Use the same approach in item 4 above for each different cause of action, even within the same question.

6. Don't cross-reference outside of each question. Be moderate with abbreviations your professor has approved.

7. Budget your time.

8. Be prepared to improvise; use the exam outline for emergences.

Chapter Thirteen

⚖ Writing a Course Paper

*[For a preview of this chapter,
see Recap 4 on p. 183]*

Typically, you won't be writing any papers for your first-year courses (except in your legal research and writing class). In your final years in school, however, you should take at least one paper course. Writing is such a vital skill for lawyers, one that pervades all aspects of their work, that you need as much experience as you can get. You also should have at least one writing sample to take with you to job interviews. If you don't publish a journal article, a class paper will come in handy for this purpose.

LEGAL WRITING STYLE

Lawyers are constantly chided about "legalese," a phrase that has come to mean verbosity and pomposity. There is a one-word response to these gripes, however, that even the most ardent lawyer-hater cannot argue with: *precision*. Yes, we would like our contracts to read as smoothly as an Elmore Leonard thriller. But it's much more important that they accurately reflect the parties' understanding. Doing this sometimes takes more words and a construction more awkward than high school English teachers would like.[1]

---

[1] I'm not going to discuss general writing style—grammar, syntax, usage, and the like. If you're a little shaky on the subject, read *The Elements of Style* by Strunk and White or any of Theodore Bernstein's books on writing.

Here's an example of the importance of precise legal writing:

Fred and Sally Jones want to sell their car to Hank and Myra Smith. Fred—who happens to belong to the Ardent Lawyer-Haters Local—says he's going to write the contract. He writes this:

Fred and Sally Jones agree to sell one of their cars to Hank and Myra Smith for $5,000. If they find anything seriously wrong within 30 days the deal is off.

Hank—a law student—says, "Hold it, Fred. There are a few questions here your contract doesn't answer. For instance: Which car exactly? Who are we supposed to pay the money to? If it's you, do you want cash or a check or a certified check? When? Who is the 'they' in the 'if they find anything seriously wrong'? When does the 30 days start running? Assuming that you meant *find something wrong with the car and not with life in general,* how do you define 'wrong'? What is meant by 'serious'? What if one of you dies or you get divorced before the sale?

Fred mutters, "Just like a lawyer. Do better if you want."

Hank pulls out his word processor and writes:

THIS AGREEMENT is made the 1 day of June, 1991, by and between Fred and Sally Jones (the "Sellers") and Hank and Myra Smith (the "Buyers").

The Sellers agree to sell and the Buyers agree to buy an orange Volkswagen Beetle, registration number 34522435 (the "Car"), for the sum of $5,000, which shall be paid to the Sellers on June 15, 1991, at the Sellers' home (the "Closing Date"), in the form of a certified check payable jointly to the Sellers (the "Check").

Upon receipt of the Check, the Sellers shall deliver to the Buyers the title document and keys to the Car.

Sellers agree that if the Car develops serious problems within 30 days from the Closing Date, then the Buyers may return the Car to the Sellers and the Sellers will refund the entire sum of $5,000. The term "serious problems" shall mean defects that cost more than $2,500 to repair provided such defects are unrelated to damage to the Car occurring after the Closing Date.

In the event that prior to the Closing Date either of the following occurs: (i) the death of any of the Sellers or the Buyers or (ii) the divorce of the Buyers, then this contract shall be null and void.

Phew. A mouthful, you think. Well, maybe. But look at the questions that Hank—acting like a good lawyer—asked. They were all legitimate concerns that both the buyers and the sellers should have considered. And because they were not addressed by Fred's contract (pristine and simple as it was), they would have to be hashed out in court should the Jones and Smith families ever have a falling out over the car. With a contract that addresses every eventuality, the parties' lawyers can determine clearly who is wrong and who is right. It would be foolish to incur the enormous expenses of a trial when the outcome is predictable.

Good legal writing buttons down every variable.[2] Consider the last paragraph of our contract. An English major might rewrite it to sound smoother:

In the event of (i) the death of any of the Sellers or the Buyers or (ii) the divorce of the Buyers prior to the Closing Date, then this contract shall be null and void.

By simply moving the "prior to the Closing Date" phrase, we have shortened the sentence and made it easier to read. But we have also drastically changed the meaning. Now, it could be read to mean that the contract will be void if the buyers get divorced before the closing date but it will be void whenever any of the four people involved dies, whether that's before the closing or ten years after—clearly not the intention of the parties.

---

[2] Good legal writing can also result in much more concise documents. Look at the capitalized terms in our example of the car contract. These capitalized terms are known as "defined terms." Lawyers use them constantly and for good reason. They can compress a great deal of information into a short word or phrase that can be used in later references. Consider this example, based on an actual legal document: *The Commerce National Bank, Inc., a Delaware Corporation; the Commerce National Holding Company, Inc., a New York Corporation; the Commerce Financial Assistance Corporation, Inc., a New York Corporation, their stockholders, subsidiaries, affiliates, partners, officers and directors, predecessors in interest, and successors in interest (hereafter called "Commerce").* The first reference to all of these people and corporations was a jawbreaker. But because the parenthetical note indicates that throughout the rest of the document we will be referring to them all by the shorthand notation of "Commerce," we can save gallons of ink and hours of eye strain.

There is virtually no end to the minuscule choices of words and phrasing that can make all the difference in the world. Note, for instance, that the use of the word "any" in "any of the Sellers or the Buyers" is proper. To use the better-sounding "either" is incorrect because "either" connotes only two units and the sentence could be interpreted to mean: "the death of either (i) both the Sellers or (ii) both the Buyers," when in fact what was meant was *if any of the four die*.

These are the finer points of legal drafting, which you will probably not learn until you are in practice. But in your early years as a legal writer, it is important to understand the importance of precision—of translating the thought into words exactly. Lawsuits—multimillion-dollar lawsuits—have been won or lost on issues as tiny as the use of one word when another was meant.

STEP ONE: FINDING A TOPIC

The first step is to find a topic. Your paper should analyze a legal issue prominent in the area of law with which the course concerns itself. This means a point of uncertainty; a conflict between or among various courts; or an aspect of the law that you find unjust, outmoded, contradictory, or nonsensical. The corollary of this comment is that your paper should not be a mere discussion of a legal rule or legal history; such a discussion rarely satisfies most professors.

How do you find such an issue? Look at the cases first—not at the law reviews or other articles. And how do you find promising cases? Examine a newsletter or bulletin dealing with the subject matter of the course. Preferably, such a publication should include a small digest of recent cases. *United States Law Week* is a good source, particularly as it presents current federal cases. "Current" is important because it suggests that the literature has not yet exhausted the topic; "federal" is perhaps more important because it is to your advantage to write about a federal issue, in contrast to a state one, because a federal law topic involves the cases in only one court system whereas a state topic could very well send you roaming through the various laws in a number of states.

Once you have found an issue on which perhaps two circuit courts of appeals have rendered different decisions dealing with essentially the same factual setting or found a single federal case by the Supreme Court or a court of appeals that you feel is subject to intelligent criticism, you have a potential issue.

Next, go to the literature—law review articles, primarily—to see if the topic has been preempted, that is, if an article already deals adequately with what you with to say. Those students or professors writing law review articles live in constant fear that, prior to the publication of their article, another author will beat them to the draw and publish an article covering the same topic.

For the purposes of a course paper, you don't need to be too paranoid. But if you find an article that takes your position and you write yours anyway, you'll be forced to make a prickly choice. If you don't cite the article and if the professor learns of its existence (and some professors *do* check sources), you may be suspected of plagiarism. Yet, if you cite the article and the professor looks it up, you won't score very high on originality. Best to pick a new topic if you can't find a different approach or can't take the opposite position from that of the earlier article.

STEP TWO: SELECTING A FORMAT

You can approach the paper in one of two ways. First, you can use the format that a law review would call a "case note" or "case comment," in which you deal primarily with a single decision that you feel is representative of an overall issue. This tack is best if the professor has set a ceiling on paper length; this case-oriented approach is more conducive to shorter papers.

Second, you might take the broader "note" or "comment" approach. The focus of such papers is the whole area of law, larger than an examination of one or two cases. You will discuss the important cases, of course, but will do so in a larger context—there will be perhaps five or six major decisions in your analysis. Moreover, you will research and cite more material from law review articles and outside sources, such as business publications and newspapers, than you would in a case-oriented paper.

STEP THREE: RESEARCHING AND ASSEMBLING SOURCES

Armed with your topic and the particular approach you wish to take toward it, buy a large package of four-by-six-inch or five-by-seven-inch lined index cards and a box to hold them in. From your initial research, you will have gleaned a number of case names and articles that deal with this subject. Write each case name, book, article, and the like on a separate card, using the style of the *Uniform System of Citation,* which you will have bought for your legal research and writing course. In the bottom left-hand corner, write R/S/O (the meaning of which will be explained in a moment).

Extracting Sources

Take the first case and read it quickly, indicating either on the card by way of page notation (if you haven't made a photocopy of the case) or circling or underlining (if you have copied the case) any good quotations or portions of the article you find to be of particular relevance to your topic. As you go through each source, you will find other cases and articles cited by the court or author either as support or as background. Some of them will be relevant for your paper. When you come to such a citation, write it down in proper citation form on a new card. When you have finished reading the case, put a mark through the R (for having "read" it), and if you have finished extracting all of the citations within the case and marked them down on separate cards, put a mark through the S (for having extracted all the "source" material). Then write a very brief synopsis of the thesis of the article, case, or book on the card.

In theory this process could go on forever, for each source will, in turn, lead to many others, but after a time you will find certain cases, articles, and books that keep recurring, and the new references and citations you find won't be relevant to your topic. At this point, you can probably rest assured that you've found the most important material.

As a final check, you should take every case that you consider to be of primary importance and "Shepardize" it. (The word "Shepardize" is a reference to *Shepard's Citator,* a listing of all legal decisions in the United States that have been affirmed, overruled, or modified by higher courts and what the citation of the subsequent case is. *Shepard's* and similar citation-checking services are now available both in written booklet form and on-line as a computer database.) Moreover, Shepardizing will let you locate recent decisions that very likely might be relevant to your theme. This procedure will be taught to you in your legal writing and research class.

As you engage in this source-extracting process, keep a pad of paper in front of you on which to jot down strategies for approaching your article, organizational outlines or suggestions that might occur to you, and any other ideas about material to add or approaches to take.

STEP FOUR: OUTLINING YOUR PAPER

Once you have read through all your material quickly, you will know in general terms what you want to say in your paper. Refer to the notes you took while reading the material and make a very broad, general outline. It might look something like this:

   I. Introduction
  II. The history of the parol evidence rule
 III. The Acme decision and progeny
     A. *Acme* v. *Bouncer*
     B. Other cases decided under the doctrine of Acme
 IV. Confusion in the courts: The problems of *Acme* v. *Bouncer*
     A. Legal problems of the case
     B. The problem from a business point of view
  V. A proposal
 VI. Conclusion

Under these headings, you will fill in your sources, using some sort of shorthand notation to avoid having to write the entire case names or names of the articles (much like the shorthand you used for your source outline). Read your source materials once again, more carefully this time. Take notes and circle passages as before to pick up thoughts that you missed the first time through. Insert the particular page citations that support your proposition into the outline. When the source is added, mark through the O on the index card's R/S/O legend (to indicate that the source has been included in the "out-line"). This will indicate that you have included the source at least once in your paper. In this way, you can easily find out if you have forgotten to include one of your major sources.

STEP FIVE: WRITING YOUR PAPER

The Body and Conclusion

Now begin to write. A tip for all writers: Don't start with the introduction; there is an urge to say too much and to be too "creative." Start with the main body and use the most un-adorned, straightforward prose you can muster. Follow your outline and incorporate material from your assembled sources.

Write footnotes on a separate sheet of paper as you go. You need not write out the footnotes fully—just a word or two to identify the source you're citing and any text you wish to include in the note itself. Every statement, whether para-phrased or directly quoted, that is not your own must be at-tributed. It is not unusual to have three or four footnotes per paragraph in legal writing.

When you have worked your way through your outline, finish with a brief conclusion.

The paper's length? The standard line from your professor is: "Why, as long as necessary." Length never makes up for sloppy thinking (writing economically is vastly harder than writing volumes). But given a good topic and a functional writing style, my advice is to write long. My only justification

for this is what I've observed: I've written short papers and
I've written long ones, and I got better grades on the long
ones. Draw your own conclusions.

The Introduction

Next, write the introduction, which should be no more
than one or two paragraphs. The introduction states the issue
or problem and your solution to it. Avoid quotations, poetry,
and other flourishes. Simply state the point you intend to
make and be done with it. (The rule of speechmaking applies
to law school papers: Tell them what you're going to tell them;
tell them; then tell them what you told them.)

Footnotes

Put all the footnotes in proper form, following the *Uniform
System of Citation* style. If you've been indicating citations in
this form on your index cards, you can simply copy the reference as it appears there into the footnote. Be sure, however, to
include what is called a "jump" citation—the specific page on
which the material you cite discusses the point you use for
support.[3]

If you added any footnotes when you wrote the introduction, be sure to renumber the remaining ones now (a word
processor will do this for you). If possible, put the footnotes at
the bottom of the page on which they appear in the text. This
is a very onerous task with a typewriter (although, once again,
a computer does it automatically). If you don't have the benefit
of high technology, it is perfectly acceptable to assemble the
notes in an endnote section at the back of your paper.

---

[3] For instance, the citation "*Jones* v. *Smith,* 250 F. Supp. 234, 246
(S.D.N.Y. 1943)" means that the case is reported in volume 250 of the
Federal Supplement series of reporters and that the case starts on page 234;
the court's statement that you are citing is found 13 pages into the case, on
page 246.

Reread and Rewrite

Once you've completed your first draft, read through it and sand down the rough edges. Then put aside the document for as long as you can—at least one or two days, preferably a week. Then read it again, aloud if possible. Do a major rewrite at this point. Question everything. Pretend you know nothing about the subject. Do you successfully explain yourself? Do your words say what you want them to say? Is your syntax awkward?

Be cruel in your critique, and prune, discard and edit wherever you think you need to. Change your entire organization if you must. Recast the sentences that are clumsy. Smooth the transitions between paragraphs and add or delete subheads if you need to.

When the typing is complete, proofread the paper at least two or three times; careless form implies careless content.[4] Make several copies of your opus for security's sake, and ship it off to your professor.

PUBLICATION, ANYONE?

If you do, in fact, follow the techniques suggested here for writing a paper, and if you write a detailed, well-reasoned article on an important topic, you might want to consider submitting it for publication in a journal dealing with the topic of law in question. Many law reviews restrict access to their pages to their own members, but there are other avenues available for students who have written high-quality papers.

---

[4] Although as you've gathered I am a staunch advocate of computers and word processors, I have to warn against too great a reliance on spell-checking systems. True, they catch misspellings and typos caused by stumbling fingers. But writers often tend to feel that running the spell-check program is the only proofreading they should perform. Spell-checkers, however, do not catch homonyms (sound alikes—"there" and "their," for instance), nor do they find accidentally omitted words or mis-chosen words that are spelled correctly ("plaintiff" for "defendant," and so on). These are by far the most common—and serious—errors in writing, much more so than transposed letters.

You should know that an actual published writing sample can greatly impress future employers.

Similarly, you might want to consider entering your paper in a writing contest (many schools and nonprofit legal organizations offer such competitions). You should, of course, check with your professor before either submitting a paper for publication or entering it in a contest.

Recap 4   Preparing a Course Paper

1. Select a topic, preferably a federal issue that is current. Be sure there is a conflict involved or an issue that will allow you to take a definite position.

2. Make certain that you have not been preempted by law review articles.

3. Begin reading the sources and writing case names and the titles of books and articles on large index cards in proper *Uniform System of Citation* style. Mark the cards with the R/S/O legend.

4. As you read, extract other sources. Make cards for each source you feel is relevant. Take notes as to what you read, or mark passages that are on point. When you are finished with a source, cross out the R and the S on the R/S/O legend. Keep a separate sheet of paper handy on which to jot notes about general strategy, organizational ideas, and other reminders.

5. When your sources start recurring and few new sources appear, you may stop researching.

6. Shepardize the major cases, and add any new cases that the process reveals and that seem important.

7. Make an outline of your article.

8. Insert into the outline a short citation for each source you'll use. Mark out the O on the R/S/O legend for that source.

9. Write the main body of the article, making short notes as to footnotes. Make your article long, but don't pad. Include

many footnotes. Be precise! Support every statement with citations to your sources. Write the conclusion.

10. Write the introduction.

11. Write footnotes in proper style.

12. Set aside the whole article for at least two or three days, then rewrite it.

13. Proofread. Carefully!

Chapter Fourteen

☙ The Complete Law School Student

THE EMOTIONAL ASPECTS OF LAW SCHOOL

You will find the study of law is an endless well and can easily absorb your every waking moment (it may pervade your dreaming moments, too!). Success in law school depends upon an unreasonable commitment to the study of law, a commitment that looms over law practice, too.

The pressures of study, the emotional abrasions of examinations, and the sheer amount of time required of you will have a marked effect on your personality. Your moods will range from despondent to angst-ridden to suicidal to elated. Free time is suddenly a rare commodity, and those unoccupied hours you can squeeze from a rock will be tainted by thoughts of assignments and examinations.

What's more, if you think you have it rough, consider your family, paramours, and friends—those victims on whom much of the burden falls and yet who don't experience the exhilaration you feel when your studying pays off, when you do well on exams, and during those moments when you realize, "I may just be a lawyer yet!"

If you and those close to you are going to survive these pressures, remember that although law is more than a career, it is not a way of life. It should not replace your personal relationships and those aspects of your being that existed before you started law school. You must rein it back continually to make sure that the law keeps its place.

Sacrifices

Something will have to give while you are in law school. Cut down on soap operas, skiing in Switzerland, football, Proust, video games—whatever occupied your time before you set to work learning torts and contracts. Consider carefully what's going to have to go, and make sure you're aware of the consequences if among your sacrifices are personal relationships or activities vitally important to you.

Statistics show that the average age of law students is now higher than it once was; many more students are married or have permanent attachments. Similarly, statistics show that there is a high degree of divorce among law school students. True, perhaps a certain dissatisfaction in personal relationships precipitates a number of changes in life-style—career changes and the choice to go to law school among them. Nonetheless, it won't take more than two weeks for those close to you to realize that you're a lot less fun to be with than you used to be (when you're around at all and not lost in the library or in your bedroom with the door closed, poring over some legal tome).

You need not sacrifice much study time to guarantee that the study of law not topple your personal life. But some of it will have to go. When you do stop studying, you should come to a complete stop. Leave the books, cases, issues, holdings, and rules all behind you. Don't let the rule against perpetuities or the defenses to slander slowly dissolve your nervous system while you are out to dinner; you might even have fun in spite of yourself.

The Benefit of Not Studying

Apart from preserving your personal life, there are two other benefits from stepping away from studying at times.

First, doing so allows ideas to gel.

Legal study is a creative process, a problem-solving process. You're continually wrestling with obstacles—not only legal problems, but difficulties in organizing your outline, coming up with topic headings, budgeting your time, and the like. Any creative activity needs a certain "baking" period, during which your thoughts have a chance to rest and solidify. Solutions will occur by themselves, but the process does not happen when the oven door is open. Close it. Go out and play. When you come back to study, your mind might have come up with a solution all by itself.

Second, maintaining contact with Earth while you're in school continues the liberal arts education that all attorneys need. An attorney is a person who must command many skills and have many interests. The most successful attorneys are those who combine concentration and masterful knowledge of law with wide-ranging minds. Because the law's ultimate concern is the relationships among human beings, a lawyer must know more than isolated rules; a lawyer must know human nature. Fortunately, that involves a far more enjoyable and informal method of study than what's presented in law school.

A story told by Oliver Wendell Holmes, Jr., justice of the Supreme Judicial Court of Massachusetts and later the U.S. Supreme Court, comes to mind. One farmer sued another for carelessly breaking a butter churn owned by the first. The local judge who heard the case looked through all his law books to find some cases dealing with churns. There were none, so the judge concluded that, there being no law on butter churns, it was perfectly all right for one person to break the churn of another, and he held for the defendant. All the law in the world won't do you any good if you're so focused on case citations and statutes that you don't have the common sense that a broad experience of life brings to you.

So study hard, yes. But practice some moderation as well— for your sake, for the sake of those close to you, and for the sake of your future skills as an attorney.

THIS BAND OF BROTHERS AND SISTERS (STUDENT ORGANIZATIONS)

An unfortunate aspect of the American legal system has been its tradition of excluding women and minorities from its ranks. This condition has been pervasive until quite recently and even now is embarrassingly slow to change.

In the last decade the percentage of women attending ABA-approved law schools rose from approximately 32 percent in 1980 to 42 percent in 1990. Minority students didn't fare quite as well. From 1980 to 1989, their ranks rose from about 8 percent to 12 percent. [1]

An evident and positive change, however, is the emergence on law school campuses of a number of student groups representing minorities. These student organizations assist their members in adjusting to legal studies; sponsor cultural, social, and political events; and serve as forums for and symbols of their members.

Examples of such organizations are Law Women, Black Allied Law Student Association, Asian/Pacific American Law Students Association, Coalition of Jewish Law Students, Latino Law Students Association, and Lesbian and Gay Law Students.

In addition to such minority-oriented groups, schools have organizations representing the student body as a whole or representing those students with a particular legal interest: a student bar association, the Law Student Division of the American Bar Association, Phi Alpha Delta legal fraternity, National Lawyers Guild (student chapters), Law Students for Public Service, Environmental Law Society, Arts and Entertainment Law Society, Tax Law Society, and Public Interest Coalition.

And, yes, some law schools actually have sports programs.

THE SWING SHIFT (NIGHT SCHOOL)

Some schools in this country still offer evening programs. The course of study takes four years, and the classes offered are virtually the same as those of the day division, albeit with some of the more esoteric ones absent.

For those of your accepted into evening divisions, I say, "Yes, it can be done." I have first-hand knowledge; I'm an evening school graduate.

[1] Note that just 24 percent of the faculty members in ABA-approved schools are women, and only 8 percent are members of minority groups.

The chasm between day and evening is not actually as great as some seem to feel. A number of day students work in law firms or in businesses although they don't put in quite the same number of hours that a night student would. Moreover, what the evening students lack in time available for studying is often compensated for by their practical business and legal experience.

On the whole, I preferred the evening classes to the several day classes I took. The students were more relaxed and more serious about their studies, and many tended to be better prepared than day students. The professors were less professorial, there were more casual discussions, and the strict Socratic approach was not used as much.

But the pros and cons aside, you're probably wondering: How will I survive? It helps if you have a job that doesn't require weekend work and that is over at 5 P.M. every night. If not, you might shop around and locate one. After your first year you might find a law clerkship or paralegal job that pays a decent salary and that isn't too demanding time-wise.

If you can trim your hours in that way, then you can follow the LCM system in this book just as any other student can. You may have to cut back on outside reading or be very selective in what you read, and your outlines may be cut to the bare essentials. But remember that you'll be taking fewer courses than the day students. They'll take six; you'll take four.

Night school isn't easy, but don't let anyone tell you that a night student can't get a legal job. Push a little harder; get the grades. Learn law. After you've been in practice for two months, no one will know or care whether you took contracts at 10:30 A.M. or 6 P.M.

CHOICES, CHOICES, CHOICES (SECOND- AND THIRD-YEAR COURSES)

Following your first year, the administration turns you loose in the candy store of curricula. You can take whatever you like. There generally are no or very few required courses during your second or third (or fourth) year. You may desire a little guidance in selecting courses.

Three influences will affect your choice:

- practical considerations (who the professor is, what time the class meets, on what date the exam is scheduled)
- personal interest in the course ("I paid tuition! I'm taking Law and Nihilist Philosophy because I want to!")
- professional considerations (what courses will give you the best foundation as a lawyer)

I tended to take courses that taught areas of law I thought a general-interest lawyer should be familiar with; I was swayed by the third influence most strongly. I was pleased I went in this direction for two reasons. I carried much of my knowledge of these bread-and-butter courses into practice with me.

I also found that these subjects were the ones that tended to be asked about on that delightful little trial by combat known as the bar exam, and by taking these courses, I found I had a head start studying for the test.

General Practitioners

So my recommendation is to shun esotericism in favor of courses that will give you a broad understanding of the profession. Those that I found most helpful were the following:

- evidence
- corporations
- wills
- an advanced practice or procedure course
- sales
- secured transactions
- commercial paper
- bankruptcy
- conflict of laws
- antitrust law
- federal courts
- ethics (this is probably required anyway)

- appellate or trial advocacy
- income taxation
- remedies

Something Enjoyable

Once you've taken core courses, peruse the catalog and take some classes just because they interest you. You might just find that a course you sign up for on a whim will so interest you that it becomes your lifelong passion.

The number of specialized course offerings has increased dramatically in the past 20 years, largely reflecting the shift toward specialization and practice-oriented legal education. While we don't yet see such specialities as the law of aerobic workouts or nouvelle cuisine law, consider the following list of courses now available that were once unheard of in traditional law school study:

- insurance law
- issuance of public securities
- Chinese law
- Japanese law
- the law of treaties
- employment discrimination
- labor arbitration
- land use regulation
- sexuality and the law
- litigation planning
- government benefits law
- federal food and drug law
- broadcast regulation
- artists and authors law
- racketeering
- injunctions
- feminist jurisprudence

Research Assignments

I would also recommend that you consider research assignments. Professors in law schools are avid writers, and schools are willing to barter academic credit for students' time in helping professors prepare current writing projects. The important considerations you must be aware of are these: (1) You must select a professor with whom you get along well because you will probably be working quite closely together; (2) the amount of work you do (huge) will not be in proportion to the credit you receive (small); and (3) the experience in researching and writing you receive can be invaluable.

Paper Courses

Finally, you must take a paper course. Writing instruction in most schools is woefully neglected; yet most of what occupies lawyers' days is writing briefs, correspondence, and contracts, or reading what someone else has written (and then, naturally, rewriting it their way). Everyone needs writing experience, and a paper course is one way to get it.

MULTIDEGREE PROGRAMS

Until recently most people who went to law school studied only law. While this is still true for the majority of students, most law schools now are offering joint degrees.

Traditionally such degrees were limited to specialties of legal practice. For instance, a number of tax lawyers have their juris doctor (J.D.) and their masters in taxation. Antitrust lawyers often have J.D.s and advanced degrees in economics or trade regulation. In many cases, however, these attorneys completed one degree first, then after working for several years in either law or their other specialty went back to school part-time to secure the second degree.

Now, however, by pursuing a joint degree program, you can relieve two degrees at once by extending your stay in school for less time than it would take to pursue the degrees separately.

Typically, you would receive a J.D. and a masters degree[2] in one of the following areas: business administration, taxation, public affairs, urban planning, trade regulation, and social work. In addition, it is possible in some schools to combine your J.D. with an M.A. degree in economics, legal history, political science, philosophy, or sociology.

CLINICAL PROGRAMS

Perhaps the most striking recent trend in law school instruction is the shift away from a purely academic, theoretical approach toward practical law.

Most schools now offer upper-class students the opportunity to work in legal clinics, assisting practicing attorneys on real cases. Under certain circumstances and with the approval of the local court system, some students are actually able to prepare real court documents and even appear in court for oral argument.

Typically, legal clinics specialize in providing the following services:

- criminal trials (defense)
- criminal trials (prosecution, in conjunction with local district attorneys)
- criminal appeals
- city government
- juvenile law
- general legal services for the poor
- human rights law
- alternative dispute resolution/mediation

[2] Normally the second degree is a designation of the school that confers it: M.P.A. in the Public Administration School, for instance. Some degrees, however, are advanced law degrees, such as the Master of Law (L.L.M.) in taxation.

YOU MEAN I GET PAID, TOO?
(SUMMER CLERKSHIPS)

After you survive your first year and return for your second, you'll start hearing rumors about on-campus recruiting, in which law firms, companies, and organizations set up shop at your school for a day or two and give you the opportunity to tell them why they should hire you.

Third-year students, of course, are looking for permanent jobs. Second-year students are looking for positions interning at firms. This apprenticeship is known as the "summer associate" or "summer clerkship" program. Most large firms offer this.

When I was in law school the summer programs were often quite luxurious. It was more of a "get-acquainted time." Interns did legal work (always under the close supervision of an associate or partner), but they also spent a lot of time being taken to fancy lunches and dinners, concerts, even cruises.

No more.

Law firms don't have that financial wherewithal to wine and dine potential employees any more. As a summer associate, you won't be given any back-breaking assignments, but you will be expected to earn your salary (which, by the way, is typically a first-year associate's wage prorated for the time employed. This year, it amounts to about $7,000 per month at a big Manhattan firm.).

Most of your work will be doing research in the library and preparing memoranda answering questions of law that arise in litigation or business deals. (For this reason, you must get some good instruction in doing computerized legal research your first year.) You also may be drafting portions of legal documents and in general preparing documents for "closings," which is the term lawyers and businesspeople use to refer to the meeting in which a transaction is finally consummated—the contracts are all signed and the money changes hands. You may even accompany partners and associates to court.

Should you try to get a job as a summer associate?

Yes. For two reasons.

First, you will get practical experience. Everything you have been taught in your first year of school is theoretical. Working in a law firm will show you how that theory is implemented.

Second, and more important, most firms extend offers of permanent employment to those who participate in the summer program. If you get along with everyone at the firm and they have the type of practice and career development profile you like, you may wish to accept this offer. It will take a great deal of pressure off you as you begin your third year, and you can concentrate on enjoying your courses or participating in moot court or on a legal journal rather than scurrying around and interviewing during the first semester. You may choose not to work in the firm you clerked for last summer, of course, but to have an offer in your back pocket is a very good feeling.

You may be tempted to go for the big bucks and send your resumes only to those firms and organizations that are prestigious. Be realistic. The market for lawyers in the early 1990s is very tight. Send out many resumes and send them to a cross-section of firms. Not everybody can work for Cravath—and not everybody wants to. A summer clerkship is the perfect opportunity to find out that you're happiest doing residential home sales or representing AIDS patients, not handling corporate financings.

Some tips on job hunting:

1. Get your resume done professionally. A host of services and books can coach you on resumes and job interviewing. When I hired people, I preferred a single-page resume that gave me the nuts and bolts:
   a. Professional experience
   b. Education and honors
   c. Where references were available
   I didn't like cutesy or long resumes. I had no need for personal information (nobody wants to know your height and weight anyway).
2. Be punctual. When your interview time is posted, write it down and be on time.

3. Interviews work both ways. Have a set of questions prepared. You have the right to know:
   a. How many years must associates work at a firm until they are reviewed for partner?
   b. How often are salaries reviewed?
   c. How many trials would you be working on in a given year and how soon does an associate get to try his or her first case?
   d. Are there bonuses for the number of hours worked?
   e. How many billable hours do attorneys work per year?
   f. Will you have your choice of specialty?
   g. How much travel is involved?
   h. Is it possible to relocate to other firm offices?
   i. What are maternity and paternity leave arrangements?

(Note, however, that an interview is not supposed to be a confrontation. If you have problems with the gender or racial make-up of a firm, there are avenues by which to challenge those inequities. An on-campus interview is not the time to make political statements.)

4. Take extra copies of your resume with you (updated from the version the firm might have reviewed several months before, if necessary).

5. Bring writing samples and any other materials that might show how you would be an asset to a firm. For instance, if you had worked for a corporation, you might show the interviewer a copy of an annual report you helped put together.

6. Don't be modest. Highlight your strengths. There is no mystery to recruiting. Interviewers are looking for people with intelligence, aptitude, drive, and willingness to work hard. Show them that you have these qualities. Class standing speaks for itself. If yours isn't particularly high, find something else that can work in your favor, such as a moot-court victory. On-campus recruiters positively love job experience; if you've worked in a business capacity before or during law school, tell them.

7. Establish rapport with the interviewer. When it comes right down to it, given roughly equal legal talent, the appli-

cant who is liked best is going to get hired. If you're going to spend eight, ten, twelve hours a day with someone, that person had better be personable and polite and have a sense of humor.

8. Be sure to write down special requests. If an interviewer wants you to meet with others at the firm or to send a copy of your journal article when it's published, jot it down. You'd be surprised how much you'll forget in the heat of an interview.

A HAND IN THE COOKIE JAR (LAW SCHOOL ETHICS)

Don't engage in any unethical activity while in school. Don't cheat on exams, don't plagiarize, and don't help anyone else do so either.

You have embarked on a career that is largely viewed by the general public as perhaps more homogeneous than it is. By this I mean that the public views individual lawyers as representatives of the *genus lawyer,* all of whose members are not appreciably different. What one lawyer does reflects on the profession as a whole, and the public probably doesn't draw much of a distinction between law students and lawyers. The general attitude toward lawyers is not always one of affection or respect. Don't add fuel to this unfortunate prejudice, which affects the entire profession, by bringing your personal ethics into question.

But ethics aside, consider the practical effects of unethical conduct. If you are caught cheating, you will without hesitation be expelled or—if lucky—be asked to leave school. If this happens, you will very likely be unable to get into any other school. Yet, if you fail a test, nothing has been ultimately affected. There isn't a law firm or courthouse in the country in which some partner or judge hasn't failed at least one course. But if you cheat and are caught, your law career will probably be over before it even begins.

If you find that certain extenuating circumstances make it pointless for you to take an exam, if you have been wholly unable to study for some legitimate reason, speak to the professor or the dean of students. The rules of school administration are often much more flexible than they appear in the catalog or school regulations. You may be able to postpone the exam or take an incomplete grade in the course until the next semester.[3]

THE 26-HOUR DAY (THE LAW REVIEW EXPERIENCE)

Not long after you begin classes, you will hear rumors about an institution within your school called the law review.

A law review is a scholarly journal published for lawyers, judges, and professors. From the perspective of their impact on and development of the profession, law review articles can be invaluable. The finest legal scholars in the country vie for space to explain why various aspects of the law should be changed, to expose injustices in the legal system, to improve the efficiency of legal administration, or to expound on legal philosophy and history. Admittedly, the articles sometimes so border on esoteric scholasticism as to make them too removed from daily practice to be helpful to most attorneys. And some articles are written not from any conviction that a legal wrong ought to be made right, but from the practical desire to publish for the prestige of it.

Yet law reviews can perform vital functions. For instance, there now exists a cause of action called "invasion of privacy." This claim did not exist as anything other than a bastard branch of the law of slander and libel until a law review article by Samuel Warren and Louis Brandeis suggested that privacy be treated as a right worthy of protection by the law of torts. Courts and legislatures listened, and the tort of invasion of privacy was born.

---

[3] If you follow the study techniques outlined in this book, you will find cheating completely unnecessary. If you do the work throughout the year, complete your outline, and never again pick it up, you will be able to get a passing grade in the course. If you can spare just one or two hours for a concentrated reading of your outline, you will very likely do better than those students who spend the entire week cramming from their class notes and canned briefs.

Professors, practitioners, and students all contribute articles to the law review. It is published solely by students, however, under the guidance of a professor-adviser, whose role is usually fairly small. A typical law review, or law journal, as it is sometimes called, is published four to six times during the academic year.

Although titles of the staff and organizational structure vary from school to school, there is usually a board of editors, overseen by an editor in chief. These dedicated souls are virtually full-time employees (and sometimes more than full-time). Often the demands on their time are so great they're unable to attend classes for much of the semester.

Below the editorial board may be assistant or associate editors, and beneath them are the members or staff of the law review. On some journals, students are provisionally admitted to the staff, but cannot become members until they publish an article and satisfactorily complete other assignments. On other reviews, once accepted, students are members whether or not they publish.

Acceptance is based on academic performance. Usually those in the top 5 percent to 10 percent of the first-year class are extended an invitation to join. In some schools, a writing contest allows those with grades not in the requisite category for invitations to be chosen for law review by virtue of their writing ability.

The function of the staff is twofold. They must write a publishable article, and they must "citecheck" or "footnote" the forthcoming articles of other students, professors, and practitioners.

Citechecking can be likened to the task of Sisyphus, the guy whose fate was to roll a rock to the top of the hill only to have it roll down again, repeating the process for all eternity. Not that citechecking is futile; you will be providing a very valuable service to the editor and authors. But it is as frustrating as can be.

This is largely because a law review article is like a massive term paper. Each premise must be supported by at least one source. The footnote will present a citation supporting the statement in the text in the very stylized form of the *Uniform System of Citation*. Footnotes will often include discussions that are tangential to the main text and that, therefore, should not appear in the body of the article itself.

Citecheckers have three jobs. First, they must check the sense and grammar of both the text and the footnotes. Second, they must check the legal content of the citations, which means reading the pages of the source cited in the article and verifying that it stands for the proposition for which it has been cited. Finally, citecheckers verify that the form of the text and the footnotes comport with the *Uniform System of Citation*.

Citechecking is what makes the concepts of the law review and free time mutually exclusive. Depending on the school and the size of the issue, citechecking may occupy up to 40 hours per week. If your school is humane, you may get academic credit for your sweat and tears.

The other task of each staffer or member on the law review is to write an article. Much of what was said about writing a paper applies to writing a law review article. There is little point in discussing the technique and style of writing for such a publication here, however, because the moment your topic is approved, you will be under the tutelage of an editor, who will guide you every step of the way.

While citechecking might be likened to a full-time job, writing an article might be compared to a full-time job plus moonlighting, at least during the formal editing process when you're preparing the article for actual publication, as opposed to the somewhat more informal research portion of the project earlier in the game. The sheer requirements of time and effort on your part mean that something will have to give. Most law reviews will relax the citechecking duty during the article-editing process. Students often miss classes during the writing period.

The law review, I feel, is a phenomenon that is largely misunderstood. Those who become members sometimes feel that this authenticates them as lawyers and eliminates the need for future study. Those who don't make it view the law review with a mixture of jealousy and resentment. Behind these feelings is the belief that only law review students get the good jobs and clerkships.

If you do make the law review, remember that it is essentially an extracurricular activity. It cannot be a substitute for an ongoing legal study process. If you don't make it, the absence of your name from the masthead will neither affect nor reflect upon your ability to be a superb law practitioner.

You should, however, *try* for the law review. If you do make it, keep a proper perspective about what the institution can do for you. Apart from raising the eyebrows of those who do not know better and filling in another space on your resume, the law review should be viewed as an intense course in legal writing and research. As such, it is far better than the sampling that you will receive in your first-year course on the subject.

Working on a review or journal also provides some introduction to the discipline that attorneys must develop. Whether you proofread or edit others' articles or write your own, you will have to be absolutely accurate. That's the way it is in practice—no typos, no overruled cases, no misspelled words, no errors at all.

Finally, it's a fact of life that the choicest jobs and clerkships await those who were law review staffers. I would like to think that this is due solely to the additional skills learned during the hours spent on research, editing, and writing and to the discipline required by the law review process. Yet the attraction is also largely due to the notions that academic scholarship equals good lawyering and that the price of a ticket to the law review is good grades. The correlation is not as clear as that, however, and law review opens career doors simply because of a prestige it does not always warrant.

But those doors *are* opened. And if it is through one of those that you wish to pass to gain entrance to the profession, whether it's a Wall Street firm, a choice public service spot, or a prestigious clerkship, you'll have to do your damnedest to make the law review, to publish an article, and to try to become an editor.

And if it simply is not your fate to be a member of the law review, continue studying at your normal pace and find other extracurricular activities. Often there will be other journals at your school in which the academic requirements are somewhat lower and which, in fact, specialize in areas of law that interest you more than the somewhat general topics usually explored in law review articles (such as environmental, urban, or equal rights law).

Another alternative to law review, especially if you think you might like to be a litigator, is to try out for moot court, an upscale version of the mock appellate argument you'll do for your research and writing class. Moot court involves interschool elimination competition, all the way up to the national level. Although moot court is aimed more at training students than at producing a legal product that is to be used by the profession, it is a far more exciting activity than the law review and equally valuable—probably more so for future trial attorneys and appellate advocates.

So, yes, the law review—and the moot court experience—can be consuming. But consider Professor Karl Llewellyn. He says this about one's involvement with law during the first year of law school:

What I am trying to write in fire on the wall is that the task before you is immense, is overwhelming, and that the official courses of the school are not enough to compass it. . . . Eat law, talk law, think law, drink law, babble of law and judgments in your sleep. Pickle yourselves in law—it is your only hope.

Chapter Fifteen

⚖ An Afterword

Law: The Institution for All Seasons

The comments, directives, admonitions ("Outline this way!" "Brief that way!") that you've worked through in this book may strike some of you as overly mechanical—as too much the tough trial lawyer's approach: apply the rules, push hard, win.

Where's the excitement, the passion, the romance of the law? In your first semester at school you have (or will) undoubtedly become aware that law is something nobler, certainly something more encompassing and challenging, than just another job. You perhaps have already started to experience a little pride when you say (or think), "I'm going to be a lawyer."

I'd like to say a few words on these feelings you may have welling up inside you and, more basically, on your relationship with the institution of the law.

Why did you apply to law school in the first place?

There are as many answers to this question as there are students. And that fact is very significant. Recall in the introductory chapter where I described how extensively law affects our lives. In the same way, law offers something for every one of its practitioners.

- Do you want material success (don't be ashamed: money, money, money!)?
- Do you want to improve our society?
- Do you want to foster capitalist institutions? socialist ones?

- Do you want to change government?
- Do you want to hold public office?
- Do you want to be a Napoleon? an Abraham Lincoln?
- Do you want to help people?
- Do you want to see people cringe before you on the witness stand?

Law can be the key to all of these goals. If you're bookish and shy, if you're petulant and aggressive, you have a place in the law. In what other profession can you be a scholar, a street fighter, a psychoanalyst? And if, like most of us, you're a composite, law will still gladly accommodate you.

But that's not all. The practice of law (and even the study of law) affects you in fundamental ways. Self-confidence, for one. You can't stand up in front of a roomful of people and talk about a legal decision and not come away with a sense that there are few confrontations in the real world you can't handle.

How about pride? A lot of people apply to law schools; a very small percentage get in. And the profession itself is a noble one. For every lawyer whose wrongdoing hits the newspaper, there are hundreds who volunteer their time to make certain that indigent and low-income clients are afforded the best legal protection in the country. And let's not forget about the typical attorney who stays in the office until 3:00 A.M. just to put a final polish on his brief so that his client has a better shot at victory the next morning.

So there you have three of the legacies of practicing law: challenge, self-confidence, pride. How about a certain sensibility that law imparts? With what premise did the introduction to this book start? That law's realm is all of life. Your practice of law will round you out and educate you in the finer (sometimes dark, sometimes saintly) aspects of human nature.

Your Commitment

These are some of the benefits law offers you. What does it require in return?

The practice of law needs more than a part-time commitment. The practice of law and the study of law, too, are like reading a legal case. Skim it once, and you won't grasp it. It will mean nothing to you. You'll feel repelled by the complexity of the facts. But plow into a case hard, pull it apart, and sooner or later it works. You have the meaning of the case, and you feel good about it.

There will be times in the next few years of study and times in your practice when you feel that opening a case reporter is the last thing you want to do. The thought of briefing a 45-page antitrust decision—oh, bring on the hot coals instead!

Then the worm gets in. You think, "Maybe I shouldn't be a lawyer. I don't feel the old first-year enthusiasm and drive any more. I'm getting lazy. I've never been as smart as everybody thought I was. I've made a wrong choice."

What do you do about these feelings?

Well, what's a lawyer's first step when confronted with any problem? To analyze it. Sort out your emotions; look at the facts. What is the kernel of the difficulty?

As to the absence of your first-year enthusiasm—good riddance! Who needs it? The first year in law school is powered by a dangerous mixture of fuel: manic enthusiasm and intense fear. You will never need to bring to the study or practice of law the effort you brought to your first year. Doing so isn't necessary. You'll learn 90 percent of the "law" you need for school in your first two semesters. The rest is just fine tuning and learning variations. So if your outlines shrink, your case briefs become skimpy, you don't begin studying until three days before the exam instead of two weeks, don't think less of yourself. By the second and third year, you'll have learned *how to* learn. You don't need to work as hard.

The Cure for Law

What about other moments of doubt, ones you can't dismiss so easily? Analyze them. What's the source? A low grade you know you didn't deserve? A bout of 16-hour days at the office? Being given assignments a secretary could handle?

These are merely temporary irritations. Time is as good a

remedy as damages or an injunction. You'll get different assignments. You'll change firms. You'll graduate cum laude in spite of the C−. You'll find a new area of law to practice in. You'll find new courses to take. And soon the discouragement is gone.

But let's say you've weeded those problems out. No, there's something else. A malaise. The blahs. You've just had it. No more cases, no more security agreements, no more stock pledge agreements, no more depositions, no more memoranda. Heaven help you if you get assigned to document discovery. And you think, "This isn't for me. It's too much. I'll go under."

What to do then?

You plow into the case. You engage in an act of faith, you might say. You turn to meet the enemy. You push hard and force yourself to read the case, digest the antitrust opinion, synopsize the law review article, draft the contract. And something curious happens. You move through your discouragement into the realm of good lawyering—a place that you can never arrive at if you skim. And the next thing you know, that discouragement turns to elation—the same twist you felt in your stomach during your first year when you grasped what you thought was an inconceivable concept.

As Professor Llewellyn writes, "The only cure for law is more law."

That then is your challenge: mechanics, discipline, and sometimes a little faith—all formidable requirements, but ultimately worth the price. You'll soon find that out. They're merely the cost of a ticket to this very remarkable land of the law, which is really what it is: a different world, a place that will welcome you, become familiar territory, make you part of it—and change you, too, just as you will bring your own skills and dedication to the profession and, in a smaller way, will alter the geography of the law.

Appendix One:
The 51 Courts: An Introduction to the American Legal System

In the United States, we have a federalist system of government. Laws are prescribed by both the federal government and the state governments. It might be said that there are 51 legal systems in the United States, one for each state and one for the federal government.

The Constitution

The extent of the powers exercised by the federal government on the one hand and by the states on the other is determined by the nation's Constitution, which is the overriding document establishing the structure and means of operation of political authority in America.

The Constitution is based on its authors' intention to create a strong, but not wholly pervasive, central authority. To carry out this intent, they made a federal government that has been empowered to act only in specified areas. Of course, these areas are quite broad, and they are made even broader by the additional constitutional provisions that Congress can make laws that are "necessary and proper" to carry out the specified powers. This provision itself has been liberally interpreted by the courts to allow Congress to enact laws that are "appropriate" in carrying out the federal government's powers.

Specifically, the major federal powers are the powers

- to regulate commerce
- to provide for national defense
- to tax and to spend funds
- to regulate foreign affairs
- to enforce civil rights

Other, specific, powers include the power to coin money and regulate its value, to regulate patents and copyrights, to establish bankruptcy rules, to operate a postal service, to regulate federal elections, and to prescribe laws governing admiralty matters. (Note that some of these powers coexist with comparable state powers, such as the ability to tax.)

Under an amendment to the Constitution, all powers not delegated to the federal government are reserved to the states. The vastness of the federal grant of power, however, leaves only a small realm of power exclusively in the states. This power includes what is generally called the "police power," which permits the regulation of criminal conduct, but— contrary to the implication of the term—is broader. It means essentially the power to make laws governing the health, welfare, and morals of the state's citizens. Additionally, state laws govern contracts; torts (personal injury, property damage, and other injuries not involving criminal laws); real and personal property; wills, trusts and inheritances; corporations; and a few other areas.

Procedural and Substantive Laws

Before we look at where the laws in this country are found, two categories into which all laws may be divided should be pointed out: procedural laws and substantive laws. You need to keep this distinction in mind when reading this book, as well as in studying the legal concepts you will be presented with in school.

Procedural laws are those that regulate the operation of the court system itself, provide the structure and mechanics of how to sue or seek an appeal, and dictate which court to go to in the first place. These laws and regulations include those establishing the time period after a harm in which someone must sue (which is prescribed by the "statute of limitations"), which courts have the power to hear particular cases, what evidence may be introduced in the trial (and how it is to be presented), how the loser in a trial appeals, and even the proper paper size and number of pages of documents to be submitted to the court.

Substantive laws, on the other hand, are those regulating social conduct in general, apart from the institution of the courts. Broadly, these are divided into torts, contracts, crimes, real property, bankruptcy, sales, secured transactions, and the like.

Thus, substantive principles deal with *what* one's rights are, while procedural principles deal with *how* one goes about enforcing them. For instance, a *substantive* rule of tort law is that if person A writes certain false things about person B, B may sue A. A *procedural* rule is that when person B commences the lawsuit, the document describing B's complaint (this document is called, appropriately, a "complaint") must include a very specific statement describing what A wrote.

Both procedural and substantive principles can make or break a lawsuit; one is no more important than the other. For instance, in the example of A and B, a court might find that what A wrote was not as bad as B claimed and so—substantively—there is no right on B's part to sue. Or the court might find that even though A's statement was clearly defamatory, B's lawyer was lazy and did not state the content of the writing specifically enough in the complaint; thus, B would be thrown out of court on procedural grounds.

Criminal and Civil Laws

You should be aware of one more distinction—between criminal laws and civil laws. Criminal laws regulate conduct in the interest of society as a whole, while civil laws regulate conduct in the interest of individuals in their private capacities. What might that mean? Here's an illustration.

Person T, a thief, steals the wallet of person V, a victim. Society, over the course of the years, has thought about similar situations and concluded that theft is not a good thing. If T wants a wallet, let him buy one; if T wants cash, let him earn it; if T wants credit cards, well, he shouldn't have left home without them.

We (society, that is, acting through the state legislature, which enacts laws) have decided that people can't simply take things from others, so we've made theft a crime. If T is caught and convicted he'll be punished—not by V, but by society (this time acting through the prosecuting attorney and the prison system). V isn't even necessary to the suit (although as a practical matter, the state may need him as a witness). The revenge, then, is the state's: *People of the State of New York v. T.*

Let's take another situation; this one illustrates civil law. Seller S and buyer B enter a contract under which S agrees to sell bolts to B. On the day they're to be delivered, S says, "I don't feel like shipping them. Sorry." The laws calls this a breach of contract. It is a wrong, though not a *criminal* wrong. But think of poor B—to her, at least, bolts are impor-tant, and she didn't get what S promised. So the law—by creating a right to sue for breach of contract—has given B a remedy. The revenge is not society's, but B's—if she wishes to go to the trouble to sue. The suit here is called *B v. S,* and the state has no involvement except to the extent that B "rents" the courtroom, judge, sheriff, and other personnel through payment of fees.

You've probably guessed that there's some overlap. In the first example, for instance, T's taking V's wallet is a crime. But it's also a civil wrong (the technical name is "conversion"). So T's action would result in two possible suits: *State v. T* for theft (criminal) and *V v. T* for conversion (civil), but these would be entirely separate. There would be different courts, different judges, different rules as to T's liability, and possibly different results (because there are different rules on liability).

Sources of Laws

Now, where are these laws found? Federal laws are all found in statutes—long booklets containing pronouncements by the federal Congress—or in rules or regulations adopted pursuant to the authority conferred by a statute. The statutes originate as "bills," are voted on by senators and representatives, and are then approved by the President. Statutes are not inviolable: they may be modified by courts (their language often is mystifying and must be examined and interpreted by judges). They may also be found to be contrary to the Constitution and thus declared invalid by courts. Every federal rule of law derives from a federal rule, regulation, or statute, however; the courts cannot originate a federal law.

The situation in the states is different. All states have their own congresses or other legislative bodies, which enact legislation. State statutes, like the federal ones, are simply pronouncements by elected representatives of the people about how one must act or refrain from acting. And, like the federal statutes, such state legislation can require interpretation by the courts and can run afoul of the federal Constitution (as well as the state's own constitution).

Yet the situation in the states is different because state law includes the "common law," a doctrine imported from the British legal system. The common law is a body of law developed by the courts, not the legislature. It involves primarily torts, contracts, and property. If you're dealing with a case in such an area of law, the rule often will be found not in a statute but in a prior court decision involving a similar fact pattern.

I say "often" and not "always" because there is much less common law now than there used to be. Statutes have largely preempted the field, and when a statute governs a matter, it takes priority over common-law rules. There are still many instances, however, in which the only source of guiding rules is the common law. Therefore, you'll have to know a little about how the system works.

A hierarchy of courts exists in each state. When confronted with a case involving one of the common-law subjects, the court will look for a decision by a higher court (i.e., one the legislature has decreed to be more powerful) in that state dealing with a similar situation. If one is located, then the lower court is bound by the common-law doctrine of stare decisis to apply the rule that the higher court stated in that earlier decision, which is called a "precedent."

In the event there are no similar decisions, the court is free to look to other states for decisions or rules to apply to the facts. It may even fashion its own rule based on public policy or the judge's own reasoning (or even—although they rarely admit it—the judge's own intuitive sense of fairness and justice).

The highest court in the state may change a rule in the interest of public policy, but courts tend to do so infrequently and would much rather simply apply the rule to a fact situation as stated in the earlier decision.

The Court Systems

Just as the sources of governing law in the United States are divided into federal and state categories, so too is the court system. The federal courts are divided primarily into three levels. The lowest level of courts—those where the trials take place—are called federal district courts. At least one such district (although usually more than one) exists in each state. Of course, even within each federal district, there are several, and sometimes many, courtrooms and judges. At the trial level there also are specialty federal courts, such as tax courts.

One level up from the trial courts are the federal courts of appeals. If the party losing a trial in a district court wishes to pay the expenses of appealing the decision, that party may do so. The appellate court looks at what happened in the trial court, may hear attorneys for the parties argue why the decision ought to be reversed or affirmed, and will then decide whether the lower court's decision was right.

The structure of the appellate system is for the most part geographic. The country is divided into multistate areas called "circuits," each of which has a single appellate court (although, once again, a number of judges).

If a circuit court has established a rule or interpreted a statute in one way, then all district courts within that circuit are bound to apply that rule when the same fact situation arises. Recall the concept of stare decisis mentioned earlier with respect to the common law? Well, the same rules applies. The circuit court, however, is not bound by the rules established by other circuits. In theory, there could be a different rule of law on a single subject in each federal circuit around the United States, assuming that each appellate court has addressed the same issue.

Above the appellate courts is the United States Supreme Court. The Supreme Court is *required* to hear only a very limited type of case—primarily only those in which the constitutionality of a federal or state statute is called into question. The Supreme Court, however, has discretionary power to hear a wide variety of conflicts (this is through the Court's ability to hear and grant petitions for certiorari, which is a formal application by a loser in the appellate court or, in a few cases, in the district court).

Because of the huge volume of litigation in this country, the Supreme Court is able to hear only a small percentage of cases on the basis of certiorari. Generally, these cases deal with important issues of federal statutory or constitutional law and civil rights of individuals, often when two or more circuits have adopted contradictory rules.

Once again, the doctrine of stare decisis is evident. If the Supreme Court has decided an issue, the rule is binding on all federal courts throughout the country and—because under the Constitution, federal law takes priority over state law—it is binding on state courts as well.

The state system of courts is similar. There are trial-level courts and some form of appellate court. But often there are only two levels (unlike the federal system with its three tiers): the trial court and the state supreme court. In addition, many states have courts of "limited jurisdiction," which means that they are trial courts that are empowered to hear only certain types of cases, such as those for divorce actions only, will and estate matters only, or civil actions seeking $5,000 or less only.

Jurisdiction

"Jurisdiction" is a concept central to any study involving the court system or procedural laws. Jurisdiction refers to the extent of a court's power to act. Jurisdiction can be defined in several ways. First, *geographically*. For instance, an Illinois court cannot generally reach outside the state and try cases involving parties or property outside Illinois unless some connection between the person or property and the state exists. Second, jurisdiction may be defined in terms of the *type* of case that a court might entertain. For example, state courts do not have the power to try federal antitrust cases. It is said that such cases are "outside the jurisdiction" of state courts.

You should not get the idea, however, that the two court systems are mutually exclusive and that state courts apply only state law and that federal courts apply only federal law. With some exceptions (such as the antitrust case just mentioned), a person can bring an action based on federal law in state court. In such a situation, the state court will be required to look to the federal rule and apply it.

Similarly, it may be possible for a person with a state claim to sue in a federal court provided the jurisdictional requirements are met (these relate to the residence of the parties and the dollar amount of the claim). In this situation, the federal court steps into the shoes of the state court in the state where the federal court is sitting and applies the law of that state.

Different courts operate by different procedural laws. The entire federal system is governed by the Federal Rules of Civil Procedure. But each state court has its own set of rules that govern the operation of the court system. Some are similar to the Federal Rules, but some are quite different. For instance, while in the federal court located in New York a plaintiff starts a lawsuit by filing a complaint with the clerk, in a New York state court a plaintiff will start the suit by serving a summons on the defendant and need not even let the court know of the action until later.

Administrative Law

The court system is not the sole mechanism for applying the law in the United States. Operating largely independently of the court system is the administrative law system. As with the sources of law and the court system, there are both federal and state administrative systems.

These involve bureaucratic agencies established to regulate specific areas of activity. Examples on the federal level (and there are usually similar agencies on the state level) are the Internal Revenue Service, the Federal Communications Commission, the Federal Aviation Administration, and the National Labor Relations Board. These organizations, under authority of Congress or state legislatures, establish rules to regulate the particular area of activity they are charged with.

All of these agencies have an internal dispute resolution process, which operates somewhat similarly to the court system. It may be possible, as well, depending on the issue raised, to seek redress in the court system instead of, or in addition to, following these administrative procedures.

Alternative Dispute Resolution

Because of the extremely high cost, both in terms of time and money, of suing someone and defending that suit, many conflicts that would otherwise have been settled through trials are now being resolved through a process known as alternative dispute resolution (ADR).

Arbitration is the best known form of ADR, but there are a number of variations on the process. We are even seeing ADR "courthouses" springing up, where the parties to a dispute, usually represented by lawyers, let mediators or arbitrators come to an equitable solution of a disagreement without incurring the sometimes prohibitive costs of a trial (which might not be resolved for years).

Throughout the 1990s, we will see more and more opportunities for people to resolve conflicts through ADR.

Appendix Two
Glossary of Legal Terms

Action: (See Lawsuit, *infra*.)

Adjudication: (See Lawsuit, *infra*.)

Affirmative Defense: (See Defense, *infra*.)

Alternative Dispute Resolution: ADR, as it is commonly called, is the settling of legal disputes by means other than a trial in court. The most common form of ADR is arbitration. As trials become increasingly expensive and court dates are extended one, two, and even more years from the date the plaintiff initially sues the defendant, ADR is being chosen by more and more complainants as a cheap, fast way to settle disputes. (See also Arbitration, *infra*.)

Amicus Curiae: This Latin phrase is translated as the "friend of the court," and usually refers to a person or organization not directly involved in a proceeding who because of a special interest or knowledge is allowed to file a brief or offer an argument in court supporting one side of the matter or the other. (By the way, Latin, the language widely thought to be practically a prerequisite to legal study, is in fact used very little in the profession. Its use is generally limited to short-hand phrases like several of those presented in this section. Botanists, doctors, and historians probably all know more Latin than the average attorney.)

Answer: (See Pleadings, *infra*.)

Appeal: The process by which the loser in a proceeding (most often the loser at trial) seeks to have that loss reversed by a separate court, whose purpose is to review the actions of the trial court and determine whether it made the correct decision. The person appealing (i.e., the loser) is called the "appellant"; the other party, the "appellee." In some cases, when the review of the lower court proceeding is based on the higher court's discretionary power to review cases of its own choosing, the loser seeking review will be called the "petitioner"; the other party, the "respondent."

Appellant: (See Appeal, *supra*.)

Appellee: (See Appeal, *supra*.)

Arbitration: A process for resolving disputes without using the court system in which the parties involved agree to submit the controversy to private individuals (arbitrators) who listen to both sides and provide a resolution to the dispute. (See also Alternative Dispute Resolution, *supra*.)

Bar: The legal profession or attorneys collectively.

Brief: The term "brief" has two meanings. First, it refers to a digest of a court opinion, prepared by students or lawyers to aid in understanding the essence of the decision. Second, it means a document prepared by attorneys for a court, setting forth the client's legal position and urging the court to accept this position instead of the opponent's.

Case: (See Lawsuit, *infra;* and Decision, *infra*.)

Cause of Action: A right to sue someone arising because that person has breached a duty owed to the one suing. Also called a "claim." A lawsuit (see Lawsuit, *infra*) may include several causes of action or claims.

Certiorari: A request by the loser in a trial or other proceeding that an appellate court review the decision of a lower court deciding against such party when that court of review is not legally bound to do so, but may in its discretion examine the earlier decision and affirm or reverse it. In contrast to an "appeal" (see Appeal, *supra*), in which the loser has a *right* to insist that the court of review decide if the lower court is correct or not. The term is pronounced "sersh-a-*rahr*-y."

Citation: As used most often in law school, a stylized notation of a statute, case reporter, or other source of legal authority. For instance, the citation of the *Jones* v. *Smith* decision, which is found on page 131 of volume 83 of the second series of New York reporters is this: 83 N.Y.2d 131 (1977). The verb "to cite" means to indicate the case or other authority in its particular form, usually as support for a statement made about the law.

Civil Law: The term "civil law" has two meanings. As used most often in this country, the term refers to the body of law involving private rights and remedies, in which the rules regulate conduct for the benefit of, and provide redress for, wrongs in favor of individuals, not for society in general. It is in contrast to criminal law. A breach of civil law gives a remedy to the actual individual harmed, and that remedy is usually in the form of a monetary payment called "damages," which roughly corresponds to the harm caused. The other meaning of civil law, when used in reference to the law of other countries, means a system of law based on the Roman legal system, in which nearly all laws were found in codes, not in court decisions. This is in contrast to the "common law" (see Common Law, *infra*).

Claim: (See Cause of Action, *supra*.)

Code: An organized compilation of individual statutes (see Statutes, *infra*).

Common Law: That body of rules of law developed by courts, not the legislature, involving primarily torts, contracts, and property. The common law is found not in statutes (see Statute, *infra*), but in prior court decisions. In contrast with civil law (see Civil Law, *supra*).

Complaint: (See Pleadings, *infra*.)

Counterclaim: (See Pleadings, *infra*.)

Criminal Law: The body of laws imposing penalties for certain types of conduct that society, acting through the legislatures of the federal, state, and city governments, has determined to be detrimental to the public as a whole. A violation of a criminal law is enforced only by the government; the victim of the crime (if there is one) does not participate in the criminal case except as a witness.

Damages: (See Civil Law, *supra*.)

Decision: The official pronouncement of a court (or in some instances another judicial or quasi-judicial body) resolving a dispute or a particular question put before it during a dispute. The term is synonymous with "opinion." These terms also refer to the printed report of the decision or opinion in a book published by the government or private publishing company and kept in law libraries. Such books are called "reporters." These printed decisions are also called "cases," although "case" also refers to the entire dispute that gave rise to the decision. Thus, if you wanted to read about a case, you would go to the library, open a reporter, and read the opinion, or decision, contained therein.

De facto: Existing in fact but not legally sanctioned. In contrast to de jure (*infra*).

Defendant: (See Plaintiff, *infra*.)

Defense: The legal reasons why a cause of action (see Cause of Action, *supra*) either does not exist as claimed or should not result in liability even if it does exist. A defense can take several forms. First, the defendant can simply deny that what the plaintiff is complaining of occurred at all (a "denial"). Second, the defendant can say that although the facts as the plaintiff has presented them are true, there is simply no law that can be applied to these facts to make the defendant liable to the plaintiff (a "failure to state a claim"; the old term to describe this position—the "demurrer"—is still used). Third, the defendant can say, "Yes, those are accurate facts, and yes, there is a law that prohibits my doing what I did, but I had a legal excuse to do so" (an "affirmative defense"). You can recall the distinction by the following:

Denial = "Not so!"

Demurrer = "So what?"

Affirmative Defense = "Yes, but . . ."

De jure: Existing according to the law. (in contrast to De facto, *supra*). In civil rights law, for instance, de jure discrimination would be a town ordinance that stated that women could not be hired to work in city hall. De facto discrimination would be an ordinance that did not specifically refer to women but had the effect of discrimination (by establishing, for instance, irrelevant height and weight criteria in hiring workers, with the result being that women were in fact excluded from the job).

Demurrer: (See Defense, *supra*.)

Denial: (See Defense, *supra*.)

Dicta: A statement by a court in a decision, which statement has no legal effect on the dispute before the court but merely expresses an observation by the court about an issue of law.

Equity: A branch of the legal system that developed hundreds of years ago in England to provide discretionary justice apart from rules of law, which—at the time—sometimes failed to result in a fair resolution of disputes because of their formality and inflexibility. Today, in this country, there are no longer any separate courts of equity as there once were, but equitable principles still exist side by side with rules of law. In general, such principles operate on the basis of a sense of fairness rather than according to an inflexible legal rule regulating conduct.

Forum shopping: The plaintiff's choosing to bring an action in a particular court, when several courts would have jurisdiction (see Jurisdiction, *supra*), in order to achieve a better chance for success at trial.

In camera: In private. When a judge conducts a proceeding in court or private chambers to the exclusion of anyone but the parties to that proceeding, the matter is said to be heard "in camera."

Judgment: The final determination by a court of the rights of the parties in the conflict before it.

Judiciary: Judges collectively or the institution of the courts.

Jurisdiction: The court's power to act. The term may refer to the geographic scope of authority (e.g., a New York court's jurisdiction extends only throughout the state) or to the type of authority (e.g., only federal courts have jurisdiction to try federal antitrust cases). Jurisdiction also refers to the court's authority over parties or potential parties to a lawsuit. If, for instance, a defendant cannot be found in the state where a suit is to be brought and has had no connection with that state, the court there is said to have no jurisdiction over him, that is, no power to compel him to appear at trial and no power to make him pay a judgment should he lose.

Jurisprudence: That branch of philosophy dealing with law and the administration of justice.

Lawsuit: The whole process of one person's suing another person in court from the first filing of papers through the end of the controversy, which is often years later. Also called a "suit" or "action." One "brings" or "maintains" a lawsuit, suit, or action against another. Lawsuits are also called "cases." The culmination of the lawsuit is the "trial," which occupies only a small portion of the whole lawsuit (most suits are in fact settled before trial). The general terms that describe resolving disputes through lawsuits and the court system are "litigation" and "adjudication."

Litigation: (See Lawsuit, *supra*.)

Majority Rule: That principle of law accepted by more than half of the jurisdictions in question when there is no uniform principle. In contrast to "minority rule." For instance, the comparative fault doctrine, which is accepted in roughly 35 states, is the majority rule; the contributory negligence doctrine, accepted in the remaining 15 states, is the minority rule.

Minority Rule: (See Majority Rule, *supra*.)

Motion: A formal request to a court—either orally before the judge or by written documents—that seeks to have the court itself, not the jury, answer a legal question or require the parties to a suit to do or refrain from doing something. For instance, before trial, the defendant will usually make a motion to dismiss the case. The judge— without consulting the jury—will then listen to the defendant's motion and decide for or against the defendant. The judge's decision is called a "ruling" (that is, the judge rules on the motion and either "grants" or "denies" it).

Party: Anyone who is formally named as being part of a proceeding. In *Jones* v. *Smith,* Jones and Smith are obviously parties, but don't let the case name fool you; there may be other parties as well. (In fact Jones or Smith might no longer even be parties by the time the case is decided; they might be dead or might have dropped out of the case. The printed report of the court will tell you who the remaining parties are and what roles they play.)

Petitioner: (See Plaintiff, *infra;* and Appeal, *supra.*)

Plaintiff: The person who commences a civil action to vindicate a wrong done by the opponent, who is termed the "defendant." When a proceeding other than a trial is involved, the person who commences the proceeding is usually called the "petitioner"; the opponent is called the "respondent."

Pleadings: Pleadings are formal documents prepared by the parties to a lawsuit that explain what the nature of the suit is, what the parties want the court to do, what the defenses are, what damages are sought, and so on. They are filed with the court and sent to all parties involved. The document that describes the plaintiff's claim is the "complaint." That which describes the defendant's response to the complaint is called the "answer." If the defendant has a claim against the plaintiff, that document is called a "counterclaim." The plaintiff's response to the counterclaim is called the "reply," although occasionally a plaintiff may reply to an answer even if there is no counterclaim. There are other pleadings as well.

Precedent: In common-law jurisdictions (see Common Law, *supra*), a precedent is an earlier court decision that is based on facts very similar to a situation presently before a court and that—because of the doctrine of stare decisis (see Stare Decisis, *infra*)—is to be considered by the court as representing the governing rule to resolve the current dispute.

Prima Facie Case: Establishing specified elements of a cause of action (see Cause of Action, *supra*) so that the law is satisfied that there is sufficient merit to the claim to require the opponent to make some effort to defeat it. For instance, the elements of a negligence cause of action are duty, breach, causation, and damages. If a plaintiff proves only three of these, the plaintiff has not made a prima facie case and the suit will be dismissed. If the plaintiff does prove all the elements, then the court lets the defendant offer excuses for the supposedly negligent conduct or show why one of the elements that the plaintiff has proved is not, in fact, present. Note that the defendant might make a prima facie showing of a valid defense, which then requires the plaintiff to rebut that showing if the suit is to continue.

Procedural Laws: Those rules that govern how the court system works and the techniques that are available by which we enforce our substantive rights (see Substantive Laws, *infra*). Also called "adjective law."

Process: The means by which a person is formally made subject to the jurisdiction of the court; specifically, those documents (such as a subpoena, summons, or arrest warrant) that order one to appear before the court or to take other action mandated by the court.

Ratio Decidendi: The legal rule in a court's decision used by the court to determine the outcome. In contrast to "dicta" (see Dicta, *supra*).

Reporter: (See Decision, *supra*.)

Respondent: (See Plaintiff, *supra;* and Appeal, *supra*.)

Ruling: (See Motion, *supra*.)

Stare Decisis: The common-law principle (see Common Law, *supra*) under which prior court decisions handed down by the same court or one with greater authority are to be applied in resolving cases based on fact patterns that are the same as, or similar to, those in the earlier decisions. Such a prior decision is known as "precedent" (see Precedent, *supra*).

Statute: A law written and approved by the federal or state legislature and approved by the executive branch of that government. In contrast to the common law (see Common Law, *supra*).

Substantive Laws: Those rules that establish our rights and impose duties upon us with respect to the society in which we live. Substantive laws are enforced according to the rules of procedural laws (see Procedural Laws, *supra*).

Verdict: The finding by the jury or judge (if there is no jury or, in a very few cases, when the judge is permitted to override the jury) as to who is the winner at trial.

Index